Warrior • 115

# Condottiere 1300–1500

Infamous medieval mercenaries

David Murphy • Illustrated by Graham Turner

First published in Great Britain in 2007 by Osprey Publishing,
Midland House, West Way, Botley, Oxford OX2 0PH, UK
44-02 23rd St, Suite 219, Long Island City, NY 11101, USA
Email: info@ospreypublishing.com

Transferred to digital print on demand 2010

First published 2007
2nd impression 2008

Printed and bound in Great Britain

A CIP catalogue record for this book is available from the British Library

ISBN: 978 1 84603 077 2

Page layout by Scribe, Oxford, UK
Index by Alison Worthington
Originated by PDQ Media,
Typeset in Helvetica Neue and ITC New Baskerville

### Author's dedication
To the memory of my mother, Kathleen Murphy.

### Acknowledgements
In the course of completing this volume I have incurred many debts of gratitude. I would especially like to thank Dr Tobias Capwell
of the Kelvingrove Art Gallery and Museum in Glasgow whose assistance was invaluable. I am grateful to Stuart Ivinson of the
Royal Armouries in Leeds and also Marie McFeely of the National Gallery of Ireland. In Paris, my thanks go to Fabrice L'Hoir,
Caroline de Lambertye and Noëlle Pourret at the Réunion des Musées Nationaux. Also in Paris, the assistance and encouragement
of Dr Nathalie Rouffiac of the Service Historique de la Défense is gratefully acknowledged.

I could not have completed this volume without the patience and help of all at Osprey Publishing and my thanks go especially
to Joanna de Vries and Kate Flintham. Finally, I owe a huge debt of gratitude to Graham Turner for the care he took in preparing
the splendid artwork for this volume.

### Artist's note
Readers may care to note that the original paintings from which the colour plates in this book were prepared are available for
private sale. All reproduction copyright whatsoever is retained by the Publishers. All enquiries should be addressed to:
Graham Turner
PO Box 568
Aylesbury
Buckinghamshire
HP17 8ZX
UK

The Publishers regret that they can enter into no correspondence upon this matter.

### The Woodland Trust
Osprey Publishing is supporting the Woodland Trust, the UK's leading woodland conservation charity, by funding the
dedication of trees.

www.ospreypublishing.com

# CONTENTS

# CONDOTTIERE 1300–1500: INFAMOUS MEDIEVAL MERCENARIES

## INTRODUCTION

The use of mercenaries in warfare has been commonplace throughout the centuries. The pharaoh Rameses II used Numidian mercenaries in his war against the Hittites in 1294 BC while both Philip II of Macedon and Alexander the Great later used Greek and Thessalian mercenaries in their numerous wars. The use of mercenaries was not unusual up to, and throughout, the medieval period and the French army at both Crécy (1346) and Poitiers (1356) included crossbowmen from Genoa in its ranks.

In Italy in the 14th century, the mercenary system reached its most sophisticated form and this was due to the unique combination of political, economic, military and social factors that prevailed on the Italian peninsula at that time. Italy as we know it today was created through the 19th-century wars of unification. However, in the middle ages the Italian peninsula was divided into a patchwork quilt of numerous independent states and princedoms. This period saw the rise of city states: vast economic powerhouses that were each supported by an agricultural hinterland known as a *contado*. In the late 13th century the population of Florence stood at around 95,000 people, which was about the same size as the population of Paris at the time. In terms of wealth, it is estimated that the kingdom of Naples alone was as wealthy as the kingdom of England.

Within city states themselves, vast changes had taken place in the military system and this encouraged the employment of mercenaries. Italian states had been in the practice of raising militias to defend their cities and the subordinate towns in their *contado*. As the political life of these cities became increasingly disturbed by factional fighting, it became necessary to entrust the state's defence to someone else and effectively disarm the local population. The beginning of this process saw several states employ an outsider, untainted by local politics, to govern their city's administration. This was known as the *podestà* system and these independent officials began to become more prevalent from the 1260s. The *podestà*'s guard, also recruited from among foreigners, was used to garrison each respective

*Portrait of a Man, said to be a condottiere*, by Antonello Da Messina, *c.*1475. The condottieri dominated the Italian military scene for the better part of two centuries, yet only a relatively small number of the major leaders have been remembered and recorded through literature, paintings and statues. This portrait in the Louvre collection in Paris depicts a lesser condottiere, the majority of whom have disappeared from the historical record. (Photograph courtesy of the Réunion des Musées Nationaux, France)

city and this guard often represented the beginning of what was to become a larger mercenary company.

So a number of factors existed to make the employment of foreign mercenaries both practical and desirable and, as the power and effectiveness of city militias decreased, the military emphasis placed on the employment of mercenaries increased. The increased use of foreign mercenaries also facilitated the ambitions of certain individuals who used the volatile and factionalized situation within their state to create their own dynasties. The officials of various Italian states had created a dangerous precedent in the 13th century when they began to appoint a single man, perhaps a nobleman, to act as the ultimate ruler of the state's affairs. These rulers were known as *signori* and prominent *signori* included members of the Este and Visconti families, who became effective rulers of cities such as Ferrara and Milan. It was in the interests of such men to use mercenaries as they could be employed to overawe troublesome state populations, not to mention state officials.

This hothouse of political, military and economic factors led to the creation of powerful mercenary groups within Italy known as *condottieri*. The funds existed to finance mercenaries and military campaigns, while such mercenary forces suited the plans not only of independent states but also of the ambitious *signori* who ruled them. Italy was, therefore, both the wealthiest country in Europe and also the most disunited, providing an ideal environment for any ambitious mercenary. The inconclusive aspect of many Italian wars meant that some states were almost constantly at war and that mercenaries had an unlimited marketplace in which they could

A contemporary painting of an Italian walled town. The governing councils of such towns employed condottieri to fight in their numerous wars, while the towns themselves were frequently the object of besieging condottieri armies. (From Burkhardt, *The Civilization of the Renaissance in Italy*).

offer their military skills to the highest bidder. The insular nature of Italian warfare also suited mercenaries and allowed the condottieri system to flourish until the end of the 15th century.

It is too easy, however, to oversimplify and classify the condottieri as mere mercenaries. Many sources, both contemporary and modern, have been inclined to do this and it is interesting to see how many recent publications do not even use the word 'condottiere', preferring 'mercenary' instead. The condottieri system was unique in terms of its time and place and was perhaps the most sophisticated expression of the mercenary ideal. In Italy, between 1300 and 1500, a professional military caste was created that was perfectly suited to prevailing trends on the peninsula at the time. The men of this caste were total professionals and were apolitical in their outlook. They developed a system of complex contracts to gain the utmost benefit from each employment. While these contracts in theory also protected their employer, the efficiency and military superiority of these men effectively held the Italian states to ransom. These men were the condottieri.

# CHRONOLOGY

Compiling a chronology of this period presents huge problems, as many of the Italian city states were almost constantly at war with each other during this period. There were also frequent incursions by the army of the Holy Roman Emperor, while Venice was engaged in a series of campaigns against the Ottomans in the eastern Mediterranean. The chronology below represents some of the major events in the history of the condottieri.

**c.1302** Roger di Flor and his 'Catalan Grand Company' sign a *condotta* (contract) to serve the Byzantine emperor Andronicus II. Credited by many with being the first condottiere.

**1326–28** Series of invasions of northern Italy by the Imperial army of Ludwig IV.

**1329–30** City and *contado* of Lucca plundered by the German Company of the Cerruglio.

Detail of a *condotta* between Sir John Hawkwood and Gian Galeazzo Visconti, Duke of Milan, dated 1 July 1385. These elaborate contracts outlined the relationship between the condottiere and his employer in precise legal terms. Many *condotte* included sub-clauses covering compensation for injury or loss of limbs in battle. (Archivio di Stato, Milan)

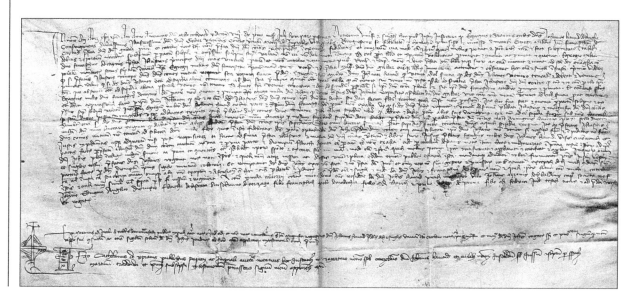

**1337** State of Florence revises its laws on the hiring of mercenaries.

**1339** Lodrisio Visconti forms the condottieri Company of St George.

**1340** Battle of Parabiago: rival factions of the Visconti battle for control of the city using German, Swiss and Italian condottieri.

**c.1342** Werner of Ürslingen forms his Great Company. Several other condottieri companies adopted that title in the decades that followed. In 1342, Ürslingen was defied by Bolognese militia and denied passage through the Val di Lamone.

**1347** The plague or 'Black Death' reaches Italy.

**1350** The condottieri forces of Milan attack Florence, heralding the beginning of a conflict that will continue intermittently up to 1392.

**1354** The condottieri company of Conrad of Landau defeated by Milanese militia.

**1358** The condottieri of the Grand Company, commanded by Conrad of Landau, defeated by Florentine militia.

**1359** Grand Company defeated by condottieri commanded by Pandolfo Malatesta.

**1360** Treaty of Brétigny ends Hundred Years War. Thousands of unemployed soldiers later flood into Italy and form 'free companies' of condottieri. The White Company formed consisting of German, Italian and English condottieri.

**1363** White Company defeats Florentine militia.

**1364** Pisan army, including the White Company, defeated at battle of Cascina by Florentines.

**1365** Company of San Georgio formed by Ambroglio Visconti. This company was mainly composed of Italians.

**1366** A league of central Italian cities formed to oppose freebooting condottieri companies.

**1367** Perugia captured by Papal condottieri.

**1368** Imperial army of Charles IV defeated at battle of Borgoforte.

**1372–73** Wars between Venice and Padua and Venice and Hungary.

**1376** The town of Faenza subjected to reprisals by Papal condottieri.

**1377** Massacre at Cesena by condottieri under Papal command.

**1378–81** War between Venice and Genoa, in which the Venetians are victorious.

**1378** Beginning of the Great Schism between the Papacy and a line of rival anti-Popes. The situation is not resolved until 1417.

**1385** Gian Galeazzo Visconti begins a long-term military campaign in northern and central Italy that continues to 1402.

**1386** A Paduan army defeats the Venetians at the battle of Brentelle.

**1387** Battle of Castagnaro: the army of Padua defeats that of Verona.

**1391** Battle of Alessandria: a Milanese army under Jacopo dal Verme destroys a French army beneath the walls of Alessandria.

**1401** Milanese army defeats the Imperial army at the battle of Brescia.

**1406** After an eight-month siege, Pisa surrenders to Florentine forces.

**1416** Battle of San Egideo: a Perugian army under Carlo Malatesta defeated by Braccio da Montone.

**1427** Battle of Maclodio: the Venetian army commanded by Carmagnola defeats the Milanese in a decisive yet relatively bloodless victory.

**1432** Battle of San Romano: Florentine forces commanded by Niccolò da Tolentino decisively defeat the Sienese army. The action was later memorialized by Uccello in a series of three paintings.

**1440** Battle of Anghiari: a Florentine army defeats a Papal army, establishing Florentine control over Tuscany.

**1478** Pazzi plot: members of the Pazzi family and their supporters attempt to overthrow the rule of Lorenzo de Medici in Florence, using the condottiere Gian Battista de Montesecco; the conspiracy is unsuccessful.

**1487** Battle of Calliano: the Venetian army defeats the Imperial army, which consists of German and Swiss troops.

**1494** French army invades Italy and the war for Naples begins.

**1495** At the battle of Fornovo a condottieri army from the allied Italian states under the command of Francesco Gonzaga opposes the army of Charles VIII of France. Both sides claim victory after a hard-fought contest.

**1500** A French army captures Milan.

**1525** Battle of Pavia.

**1526** Death of Giovanni delle Bande Neri, last of the great condottieri.

**1527** The sack of Rome by the Imperial army of Emperor Charles V.

# ENLISTMENT

The term condottiere literally translates as 'contractor' and derives from the *condotta* or contract that defined the agreement between mercenaries and the Italian state or princedom that employed them. It is now generally used to describe the leaders of bands of condottieri, or contractors, but technically speaking any mercenary who signed a *condotta*, or was included in the terms of a *condotta*, can be referred to as a condottiere.

While several mercenaries were later credited with the title, according to the Florentine chronicler Giovanni Villani the 'father of all condottieri' was Roger di Flor, who was born in Brindisi in the mid-13th century. He initially enlisted in the service of the Holy Roman Emperor, Frederick II, before serving with the Knights Templar. Around 1302 he travelled to Constantinople with his 'Catalan Grand Company' and signed a *condotta* to serve the Byzantine emperor Andronicus II. Like so many condottieri that followed him, he was soon more powerful than his employer and embarked on a campaign of self-enrichment. In 1306, in a fatal lapse of caution, he allowed himself to be lured to a supposedly friendly meeting with his employers, where he was assassinated along with his escort. In many ways it could be argued that this 'proto-condottiere' set the tone for the men who followed in this profession; not only in his methods but also in his relations with his employer.

Filippo Scolari, otherwise known as 'Pippo Santo', a native of Florence and a condottiere who exported his talents and served Sigismund of Hungary. He is depicted in a mural by Andrea del Castagno in the Villa Carducci, Florence. (Author's photograph)

The true condottieri system had its genesis in the 13th century as increasing numbers of foreign troops crossed the Alps into the Italian peninsula in search of employment. By the early 1300s, there were numerous mercenaries in Italy and these consisted of Germans, French, Catalans and Swiss, among others. They were led by accomplished knights such as Werner of Ürslingen (d. 1354). Native Italian condottieri such as Castruccio Castracane (1281–1328) were extremely rare among this first generation of condottieri.

Following the Treaty of Brétingy in 1360, which ended the first phase of the Hundred Years War, a large number of unemployed soldiers travelled to Italy to seek employment in the armies of the city states. These men now included significant numbers of English and they often banded together in free companies. Under an elected captain they then offered themselves for hire. These mercenary units included the White Company, the Black Company, the Company of the Flowers, the Company of the Star and several companies of St George. While foreigners were in the majority in these early condottieri companies, from the 1370s an increasing number of Italians began to serve as condottieri, and they in turn came to dominate the condottieri system. The later condottieri of the 15th century contained in their ranks a large number of men from the poorer regions of Italy.

In essence the condottieri system was defined by the elaborateness of the legal contracts that controlled these mercenary arrangements. The sophistication of these mercenary contracts led to the evolution of a military system that was unique to medieval Italy. One

A mid-15th-century memorial medal of Niccolò Piccinino (d. 1444), the son of a Perugian butcher, who became a leading condottiere. He was succeeded by his two sons, Jacopo and Francesco Piccinino, who both grew up to be condottieri. (Private collection)

could over-simply and define 'condottiere' as a mercenary who fought for pay, but the condottieri system was an extremely nuanced one. The condottiere was an absolute military professional who served his employer without any considerations of nationality, ideology or wider political allegiances. In the businesslike atmosphere of medieval Italy, it is perhaps not surprising that the contracts that governed the employment of condottieri were intricate and legalistic. The terms of these contracts can be seen as being mutually binding and beneficial but, as the condottieri held the balance of military power, one could argue that these contracts were biased in favour of the mercenaries.

By the 15th century, the terms of such contracts had achieved a certain level of uniformity. For an agreed sum, the condottiere agreed to serve his employer for a fixed period. An advance was usually paid and further payments came in instalments. The contracts included insurance clauses and compensation for serious injury or loss of limb. In 1446, for example, a condottiere in the Venetian service named Ferrando da Spagna was offered a pension of 6 lire a month having lost his right arm in battle. He preferred to take a lump sum of 40 ducats and remain in service. It was often stipulated that the condottieri were to be allowed to buy their food at preferable rates when not on campaign. Contracts also covered the issue of captured plunder while on campaign; the condottiere was allowed to keep all plunder taken in enemy territory and also all arms, armour and equipment captured from defeated troops. Additionally, there were sometimes special clauses that offered bonus rewards or rights of citizenship to condottieri who exhibited bravery in battle. Finally, many

*condotte* included a final payment, in return for which the condottiere agreed not to work for his employer's competitors for a certain period after the expiration of his contract. In any business terms, this arrangement can only be seen as a good deal.

What then did the condottiere supply in return? Firstly he was required to provide a certain number of fully equipped men, usually a mixture of cavalry, dismounted men-at-arms and archers or crossbowmen. This force had to be kept well trained and equipped and had to be ready to be deployed by the employing state at a moment's notice. In doing this, the condottiere fulfilled his primary function. If he was successful on campaign, any captured castles and estates reverted to the employer and the condottiere could keep portable property only. The condottiere was also obliged to keep his men in good order while on friendly soil and was to stop looting and violence towards civilians.

Within condottieri armies, the basic unit of organization was the 'lance'. While there were variations within different condottieri companies and bands, a lance usually consisted of a mounted knight, a squire, a page and two archers or men-at-arms. Each lance therefore consisted of five men, and the condottiere would contract to provide a certain number of lances to serve his employer. As the condottieri system developed, the number of lances controlled by the more powerful condottieri increased in number. In 1441, the band of the condottiere Micheletto Attendolo consisted of 561 lances or over 2,800 men.

The rates of pay of individual condottieri varied greatly throughout this period. Taking the Papal army as an example, in 1371 Pope Gregory XI was paying 18 florins per lance per month. This had been reduced to 15 florins by 1404 and, as the market flooded with potential condottieri, by 1430 the rate had slumped to just 9 florins per lance. Initially it was the practice to pay the leader of the condottieri company, on the understanding that he would then pay his men on a monthly basis. This system was open to abuse as the considerable sums passed over to condottieri captains represented a huge temptation. For example, in January 1364, the famous English condottiere Sir John Hawkwood was given 150,000 florins by Pisan state officials to cover six months' wages for his men. While Hawkwood had a reputation for dealing fairly with his men, other condottieri were less scrupulous and withheld their men's pay for their own use. It therefore became more popular to pay each condottiere a fixed sum each month, and by the 15th century this process was often overseen by state officials or *collaterali*.

The *collaterali* ultimately became extremely important figures in the condottieri system as it was up to them to defend the state's interest and see that the terms of each contract were filled. It would appear that initially they were appointed on a temporary basis to oversee each individual contract. By the 15th century, powerful condottieri such as the Viscontis and Sforzas, who eventually became successive rulers of the state of Milan in their own right, employed permanent *collaterali* to oversee the daily administration of their mercenary armies. The *collaterali* were responsible for the supply of food and weapons as well as the payment of wages. They also organized inspections and musters to ensure that their employer was receiving the number of troops that he was paying for. In 1468, one *collaterale* inspecting condottieri in Papal service found that one cavalry unit was 13 horses short of its contracted strength of 200, while an infantry company was short by 12 men. On discovering deficiencies in men, horses or equipment, the *collaterali* could then levy fines on behalf of their employers. As a consequence, the *collaterali* became increasingly important. By the late 15th century, powerful condottieri employed permanent *collaterali* to oversee the daily administration of their mercenary armies, and by the latter part of the century these men were responsible for recruiting, discipline and even obtaining intelligence about military movements.

Despite this high level of control, the condottieri system was open to abuse. Some states gained a reputation for being tardy in the matter of payment and this often provoked threats of desertion or defection by condottieri. In terms of actual sums paid, Florence gave the best rates, while both Milan and Venice gave poor rates of pay. In general, however, the system worked well and was constantly developing throughout this period. While the condottieri company had begun as more or less the property of its captain, by the end of the 15th century, states were recruiting soldiers directly. Although the armies might be commanded by officers who were condottieri, these changes in recruitment policy predicted the rise of professional standing armies.

# TRAINING

Technically speaking, all of the early condottieri were trained men. Their military prowess and experience was what made them a desirable prospect for their future employers. It was their skill at arms that led state officials to decide that employing condottieri was a better practical and financial option than raising and training their own troops. This was true of all the early condottieri of the 14th century as the majority of them were experienced veterans of the Hundred Years War. Each one of them, whether he was a mounted knight, a dismounted man-at-arms, an archer or a crossbowman, was expected to be able to fulfil a military role and also to maintain his own weapons and armour.

The terms of condottieri contracts stipulated that the condottiere should provide a company of trained and fully equipped men. These companies were subject to an inspection by state officials that would have ascertained the men's level of training. Throughout this period therefore, condottieri captains preferred to recruit men who had already achieved some level of skill at arms. Yet some system of training would have existed to maintain a population of trained condottieri.

The first method employed was to train the young men who served as squires and pages within condottieri companies. These young men joined a company in their early teens and initially acted as servants to the older and experienced condottieri. It is likely that they frequently followed other members of their family into the company, perhaps their fathers, uncles and older brothers. Within their own condottieri company, their training would begin.

Those destined to serve as cavalry would be taught to ride proficiently and also how to care for horses. They would take care of their masters' armour and weapons. In helping to arm condottieri before a review or battle, they learned how to wear armour correctly and what types of armour gave the best protection. Interspersed with this practical education, they were also taught how to fight with both sword and lance.

A heavily armoured Venetian cavalryman as depicted in Cesare Vecellio's *Habiti antichi et modernii di tutti il Mondo.* Although published in 1598 it gives a good indication of both the type of armour and the embellishments used by later condottieri. (From Men-At-Arms 210: *The Venetian Empire, 1200–1670*)

Not all young squires and pages were headed for the cavalry force and others would have been attached to dismounted men-at-arms and infantry. They too would have been taught how to use and care for their arms and equipment. Some men would have been destined to become archers, crossbowmen or artillerymen, and they would have undergone a more intensive training to turn them into skilled exponents of their profession.

In battle, such young men had an actual combat role. Some would take care of spare horses or hold the horses of condottieri who had dismounted to fight. Others would support the infantry, perhaps bringing forward water to refresh them and also carrying spare weapons, arrows and crossbow bolts. It is likely that they would have remained close to the men of their own 'lance' and would have helped to remove their own wounded from the field. Some medieval accounts also refer to young squires and pages being allowed to dispatch the enemy wounded.

An early 15th-century illustration of crossbowmen in action. One is shown operating a windlass winding mechanism, and both wear leather jerkins as some form of protection. Mercenary crossbowmen made an early appearance in medieval armies and were a standard feature in condottieri companies. (From Men-At-Arms 113: *The Armies of Agincourt*)

From the surviving accounts of the lives of the condottieri, it is also obvious that, apart from this basic apprenticeship into the condottieri profession, some young men were recognized as being of particular promise and were selected for further training. This was especially true by the 15th century when life as a condottiere represented a valid career option for a young man. Rather than joining the Church or studying to be a surgeon or advocate, a youth could choose to train to become a condottiere.

Many of the successful condottieri of the 15th century trained under renowned exponents of the profession. Francesco Novello Carrara, one of the victors at Castagnaro in 1387, had been apprenticed as a young man to Sir John Hawkwood. Jacopo dal Verme learned his profession under Gian Galeazzo Visconti and assisted his mentor in the coup that made Visconti the duke of Milan.

Some of the more successful condottieri leaders established what were de facto schools of the condottieri profession. Here they taught their young pupils not only skill at arms but also tactics and the practical knowledge that they would later need to negotiate contracts and maintain their own companies. Condottieri leaders such as Alberigo da Barbiano (d. 1409) and Bartolomeo Colleoni (d. 1475) trained a whole series of young men, who first served as their junior officers before becoming leaders of their own companies.

To be a successful condottiere, a captain relied on skilled men who continued to train to hone their fighting prowess. The condottieri captain who paid attention to such details usually reaped the rewards in battle.

Different leaders put an emphasis on different aspects of their men's training dependent on their tactics in battle. Some preferred to dismount their men and use them in tight infantry formations. If they wanted their men to be supported by the fire of archers or crossbowmen, this required different training and coordination if it was to be done efficiently.

Generally Italian warfare of this period was characterized by the employment of large numbers of armoured heavy cavalry. Alberigo da Barbiano was a renowned exponent of heavy cavalry tactics and many condottieri leaders followed his example. The successful deployment in battle of large numbers of cavalry must have required constant training. It took a considerable level of skill and nerve to advance on an enemy in a tight, knee-to-knee formation, what was later referred to as 'en muraille'. Such formations could not rely on the mere instinct of a supposedly trained condottiere. To achieve success, a condottiere had to engage his men in intensive training before they joined battle with the enemy.

The training of condottieri was therefore an ongoing and intensive process. The pool of condottieri was constantly being renewed through the instruction of young men in the ways of the profession. The more promising, wealthy or ambitious young men could receive a further level of higher education under a renowned condottiere before taking command of their own companies. On a purely practical level, the success of condottieri in battle was directly proportional to the level of training in which they had engaged in order to perfect battlefield manoeuvres and formations. So while a *condotta* might stipulate that only trained men could be employed, in reality there were various levels of training going on at all times within condottieri companies.

A detail from Simone Martini's 1328 fresco entitled *Guidoriccio da Fogliano* in the Palazzo Pubblico, Siena. It shows a fortified town with a military encampment outside. Cities that employed condottieri preferred to have them billeted outside the city walls. While this represented an expense in itself, it was preferable to dealing with the problems associated with condottieri, even friendly ones, when they were on the prowl within cities. (Author's photograph)

# DAILY LIFE

When not on campaign, the life of a condottiere had the potential to be quite pleasant. In general, condottieri captains had to be responsible for billeting their own men and the practice was not to have quarters in large towns. They might, however, live in smaller towns or villages near the capital of their employer. It later became normal practice for condottieri to gather in large tented encampments near the capital of the state that was employing them. During the 14th and 15th centuries therefore, such large encampments would have been a relatively common sight near cities such as Milan, Florence, Pisa and Rome, as these were some of the main employers of condottieri. When in camp, each condottiere provided his own shelter. For a lowly foot soldier this could be simply a basic shelter or he might just sleep wrapped in his cloak. The better-off condottieri captains had the means to provide themselves with tents, and paintings of the period show condottieri encampments as small cities of highly coloured tents.

It is also probable that the men of specific lances bought or acquired tents for their own collective use. In wintertime, a special officer, usually with some experience of basic field engineering, was assigned to provide more substantial quarters for the men.

The terms of the mercenaries' contracts stipulated that they should either be fed at the state's expense or be allowed to buy food at cost prices. The prospect for a condottiere 'at rest' was therefore quite appealing as he could acquire food and drink at cost price at most. As has always been the case with commissariat arrangements, such contractual obligations were not always honoured. Florence seems to have had a particular reputation for being miserly in this respect and one 15th-century condottieri captain commented that:

> The Florentine officials sell victuals at the dearest price possible, without any concern for the regulations concerning prices and quality; the money is so debased that it buys very little; and if provisions are sent from Lombardy or elsewhere these Florentines make us pay a duty on them or keep them for themselves.

The responsibility for maintaining discipline and order among a condottieri army in billets fell to the *collaterale* and his lesser officials. The *collaterale* was responsible for maintaining the men from his company in billets or in a tented encampment. It was up to him to supervise the digging and use of latrine areas and the construction of the encampment and he also had to oversee the supply of food and drink. He had to impose discipline and prevent desertion and in this he was assisted by a provost officer. Some condottieri armies even travelled with their own executioners.

Such condottieri encampments of course attracted large numbers of camp-followers and hangers-on, many of them of varying degrees of usefulness. There were surgeons and barbers (often men serving in both capacities), priests and friars, out-of-work condottieri and also the ubiquitous prostitutes, thieves and beggars that followed in the wake of all military formations. A condottieri encampment had the potential to become a microcosm of the seamier side of medieval life.

A depiction of soldiers, possibly condottieri, assaulting a woman. Such practices were common and led to state officials billeting condottieri companies outside towns. (Fresco of about 1340 by the Lorenzetti brothers in the Palazzo Pubblico, Siena. Author's photograph)

It is not surprising, therefore, that the states which employed them did not want condottieri lounging around in camp near the walls of their own capital. Condottieri were often forbidden from entering the walls of major cities as they had a tendency to steal from the citizens and also to assault them. The city fathers of employing towns were also concerned about their womenfolk, and the practice was to send young women to secure towns away from where the condottieri were quartered.

While such preventative measures may have protected the employer from theft, assault and the abuse of the local women, the idea of having large and inactive condottieri armies was still unattractive. Inaction resulted in indiscipline, and condottieri captains often realized this themselves and conspired with city officials to create a series of false alarms that would take their army into the countryside in pursuit of a supposed enemy.

Also, paying and providing for a condottieri army to remain in camp defeated all financial logic. The condottieri's contracts usually stated that they had to be paid extra if they carried out guard duties within the city or in surrounding towns. For an employer, therefore, paying and maintaining a condottieri army in camp represented a large expense with little prospect of a practical return. It was in the employer's interest to send condottieri armies into the territory of the enemy; this in itself was an effective means of waging war, as the condottieri army would ravage the enemy's countryside in an effort to sustain itself.

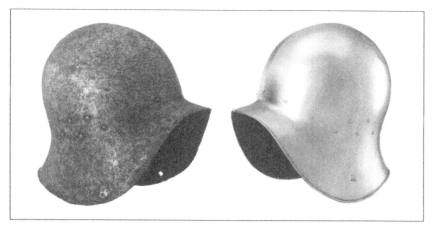

A mid-15th-century Italian sallet helmet, possibly made in Milan. The sallet to the left is the original and it is contrasted here with a modern reconstruction on the right. A series of holes in the skull of the original helmet suggest that it was later modified with a handle and used as a cooking pot or coal scuttle! In its original use, it offered good basic protection and is of a type used by condottieri infantrymen. (Royal Armouries, Leeds)

While a condottiere might find camp life fairly appealing, he was in general unlikely to have had a long period in which to enjoy it. The imperative to engage in some form of action to offset the expense of the employers would eventually force his commander to take his men on a campaign against the enemy. The 14th and 15th centuries were also times of periodic famine and disease. Food shortages and the transport difficulties encountered in wintertime often reduced condottieri camps to assemblies of the starving. The fact that so many people lived in close proximity while in camp often resulted in the outbreak of diseases such as cholera and typhus, while the plague, or 'Black Death', that swept Europe in the mid-14th century struck down condottieri as well as civilians.

The successful condottiere commemorated: Guidoriccio da Fogliano as he appears in Simone Martini's 1328 fresco in the Palazzo Pubblico in Siena. Fogliano had recaptured two towns that had rebelled against the authority of Siena, and was honoured in this fresco, which shows him riding richly accoutred and carrying his baton of office. (Author's photograph)

However, in general, life in camp held far more attractions for a condottiere than the prospect of going on campaign. When pay was in arrears, a refusal to leave camp was often used as a tactic to ensure the payment of wages. It was perhaps typical of the condottieri to turn the issue of their maintenance in camp into a weapon that they could use against their employers if their payment became irregular.

## APPEARANCE AND DRESS

Just as is the case today, in the 14th and 15th centuries styles came and went, and contemporary illustrations show a wide range of different civilian forms of dress. When not armed for duty, a condottiere's dress would have reflected civilian styles.

Both fashion and etiquette demanded that men keep their heads covered. Illustrations of the period show many different styles. The most basic was a simple white linen skullcap, with a drawstring to tighten the hat over the ears. Others were quite elaborate, with fur rims, and many had elongated crowns which allowed for the hat to be worn with flaps or cones suspended over the brim. Some funeral murals, especially those of Sir John Hawkwood and Niccolò da Tolentino, depict condottieri wearing large hats which were in the style of an oversized beret. Hoods were also common, either as part of other garments or as separate items in themselves, and these often extended over the shoulders.

A modern reconstruction of a suit of Italian armour of the late 14th century. Made by Peter Wroe, it is in the collection of the Royal Armouries, Leeds. This suit is typical of the period and is based on items in the Churburg Collection in Italy. It incorporates a bascinet helmet and plate defences for the legs and arms, while a breastplate and mail cover the torso. (Royal Armouries, Leeds)

Over a linen shirt, a condottiere would wear a tunic or doublet. One of the most common styles was the *perpunto*, which incorporated a form of soft padded armour. The length of tunics varied over this period. It was not uncommon for civilian doublets to ape military styles and therefore some included false arming points. On his lower half, a condottiere would wear hose. These came in two pieces and each hose leg was secured separately to white linen undergarments. For the more fashion-conscious condottiere, this practice allowed him to wear two different-coloured hose. In some cases the sole of the foot was reinforced with a leather strip.

Some shoes of this period survive in various museums across Europe and they display many different styles. Ankle boots were worn and also longer boots for riding. There were also numerous different types of leather shoe. What strikes a modern observer most is perhaps the thinness of these shoes and their seeming unsuitability for any street conditions, let alone medieval ones.

Finally, as an overgarment, a condottiere would wear some form of cloak. These were often quite simple affairs. For the more affluent condottiere, they could incorporate some form of fur trim or lining. Surviving illustrations, such as the Fogliano wall mural in Siena, show condottieri captains bedecked in luxuriant cloaks of many colours.

Italian armour developed constantly throughout the 14th and 15th centuries. The armour of the early condottieri was of relatively simple design. The majority of the first generation of condottieri were non-Italians; they included Germans, Swiss, English, French and Catalans, among others, and they used a style of armour that had proved effective during the Hundred Years War. Helmets were often a variation of some form of helm. These helm-type helmets followed a very straightforward design but occasionally they included a visor. Beneath this a condottiere could also wear a simple bascinet with a mail aventail to protect the neck and shoulders. Many condottieri just wore a simple, open-faced helmet as head protection (see Plate A).

These early armours included various items for the protection of arms and legs. The most simple method was to use mail arm coverings and leggings. Over these, further arm defences and leg greaves could be

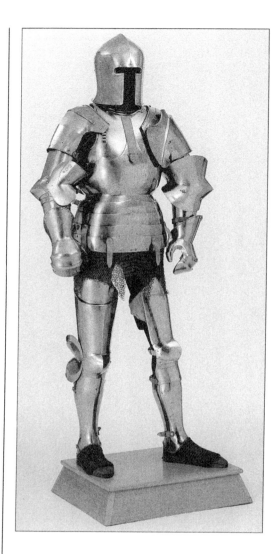

worn and these could be made of reinforced leather or metal. A prudent condottiere would also protect his hands with mail gauntlets, which could include metal plates. Feet were covered with mail and this could also be reinforced with metal plates or scale-type armour.

Much attention was given to protecting the torso. It was common to wear a mail hauberk, and over this a leather coat or apron, lined with metal plates, was also worn. During this early period, condottieri still carried a shield as a further form of protection. While this kind of armour was mostly used by men-at-arms for mounted and dismounted combat, further forms of armour were used among the lesser infantrymen, archers and crossbowmen. These armours had to offer good protection but still allow a great deal of movement for the user. A common and simple form of armour included a basic steel helmet and also a mail shirt or a steel-plate-reinforced leather brigandine. This form of armour can be seen in surviving illustrations of the period. From the middle of the 14th century, some infantrymen used a steel-buckler-type shield as a further form of protection.

The condottieri are usually equated with heavily armoured horsemen and it is true that there were huge developments in armour throughout this period. The 14th century saw the increasing use of plate armour and this was used in combination with mail armour. Helmets developed to a great degree and various types of visored bascinets were employed. By the late 15th century Italian armour had reached high levels of sophistication and workmanship. Developments in projectile weapons had reached such a degree that it was deemed necessary to virtually encase condottieri in complete suits of jointed plate armour. Shields had been gradually abandoned for mounted combat, and suits of armour included exaggerated protection on the wearer's left side, usually in the form of an elaborate gardbrace over the left shoulder and neck.

Despite the developments in plate armour, for extra protection Italian condottieri still wore large amounts of mail. It was not uncommon to wear a mail shirt and a mail skirt under a suit of plate armour, while extra mail sections extended over arm and leg protection. Feet were covered by mail or metal sabatons while the hands were encased in elaborate gauntlets. Visored armet-type helmets had been developed to protect the head, and some form of leather or metal arming hat would be worn underneath these (see Plate H).

Such developments in armour protected condottieri quite literally from head to toe. Armourers constantly sought out new ways of increasing protection. These included developments such as the features of the Maximilian style, which incorporated fluted ridges all over the armour and helmet in the hope that they would dissipate the force of blows.

The horses of these armoured condottieri also had to be protected and the bard or horse armour was developed, which provided protection for the head, neck, chest and flanks of a condottiere's mount.

Some sources refer to condottieri companies as polishing their armour to a high degree. The bright burnished armour was allegedly the reason behind the naming of the White Company in the 1370s. Contemporary illustrations seem to contradict this idea, as condottieri armour is often shown as being painted black, which would certainly have made it more easy to maintain in the field.

Alongside the armoured horsemen, condottieri armies still included other types of infantrymen. Whether they were archers, crossbowmen, handgunners or heavy and light infantrymen, they wore some form of protection. Open-faced helmets were common, and padded or plated brigandines were also worn. Some of these infantrymen could afford a metal back- and breastplate, while some heavy infantrymen wore metal leg protection on their left, or leading, leg. Shields of varying sizes were used, the largest and most cumbersome being used by crossbowmen when firing from a static position.

In terms of both civilian dress and armour, the appearance of the condottieri changed dramatically throughout the 14th and 15th centuries. While illustrations of civilian clothes often seem to represent somewhat foppish and impractical garments, in terms of armour and equipment the condottieri were becoming increasingly better protected throughout the 1400s. This was especially true in the case of the mounted heavy cavalry, who must have appeared as terrifying men of steel when on campaign.

## BELIEF AND BELONGING

In any work about mercenaries, it seems to be almost a contradiction to discuss issues such as belief and belonging. As each condottiere was motivated by profit, how could such issues affect his behaviour or attitudes? Nevertheless, the complexity of condottieri attitudes to business and warfare was also reflected in their approaches to other more human issues.

Every condottiere was, at least nominally, a Christian. To be more specific, in the pre-Reformation era, he was a Roman Catholic. How this Catholicism might affect the daily life of a condottiere is open to some debate. It is likely that most condottieri attended mass on occasion and also obtained the sacrament of confession when possible, especially when a battle was imminent. Like most medieval men and women, he would have held very straightforward views on God and the possibility of divine intervention and he would have wished to obtain some form of a state of grace before going into battle. In practical terms, it would appear that condottieri companies employed their own chaplains to travel with them and also used local churches while on campaign.

As with all aspects of condottieri history, all of the above comes with numerous caveats. This is most apparent in the condottieri attitude to Church property. Churches, convents and monasteries were repositories of wealth and were therefore plundered. Also, the men and women of the Church, be they priests, monks or nuns, were not safe from the violent attentions of condottieri. In medieval warfare, plundering churches in enemy territory was seen as an acceptable tactic, but condottieri also occasionally engaged in such behaviour while on friendly ground. Moreover, it is even recorded that Italian mercenaries (whose number included former condottieri) fought in the army of Mohammed II during

OPPOSITE PAGE **A suit of Gothic field armour, more commonly known as the 'Avant Armour', dating from about 1440. This exquisite suit of armour was made by members of the Corio family in Milan and is the oldest near-complete suit in the world. It is now on display in the Art Gallery and Museum at Kelvingrove, Glasgow. Neither the helmet nor the left gauntlet are original to the suit but nevertheless it represents the height of the armour-maker's art. The word 'avant', meaning 'forward', is repeated as an inscription on the breastplate and this gives the armour its name. Various religious inscriptions are also included on the armour, obviously intended to protect the wearer in battle. (Photograph courtesy of the Art Gallery and Museum at Kelvingrove, Glasgow)**

The tomb of the tyrannical Sigismondo de Malatesta (1417–68) in Rimini. During the course of his brutal career, Sigismondo served as both a condottiere and lord of Rimini (Author's photograph)

the sack of Constantinople in 1453. Presumably such men did not feel constrained by their religion whilst fulfilling their contract to the Sultan.

Thus, though he was in theory a Roman Catholic, the people and property of the Catholic Church could fall victim to a condottiere's worst instincts. In his defence, though, it should be remembered that such behaviour was commonplace.

It could equally be argued that all medieval mercenaries ultimately rejected any true sense of belonging in their pursuit of financial reward. However, it is apparent that the condottieri did entertain ideas of belonging and that these loyalties revolved around their own condottieri company. While an individual condottiere might move from company to company, it made economic sense to attach oneself to a particular company for a long term. The bigger and more effective the company, the more lucrative its contracts would be. The 14th century was the era of the great condottieri companies. These were made up of foreign mercenaries and their associated servants, womenfolk and also other assorted hangers-on including doctors and priests. Some historians have ascribed a certain nobility to these companies, referring to them as 'companies of equals'. In all probability this concept is extremely naïve. It is more realistic to state that these 'free companies' evolved around a strong and effective leader and grew in size with each success. In terms of belonging, it was sensible for a condottiere to become associated with one of the great companies such as the White Company or the Company of St George. In this respect, the idea of belonging was inextricably linked with success on the battlefield and the subsequent reward for that service.

However, as Italian-born condottieri began to dominate the mercenary market during the 15th century, a more sophisticated concept of belonging evolved. This was based on the concept of the *casa* or household, and the system was a strictly hierarchical one. A condottiere captain could be a member of the lesser nobility or, again, a condottiere who had enjoyed a certain amount of success. Around him, he would gather his *casa*, which consisted not only of knights and men-at-arms but also of *collaterali*, trumpeters and other servants. This *casa* or household formed the nucleus of his military strength and further forces could be gathered around this central unit, increasing the condottiere's potential and enabling him to serve as a captain-general of a larger army.

There was a semi-feudal aspect to the *casa*, as the leader was often an independent ruler in his own right. He would include the sons of his subjects in his *casa* and thus ensure loyalty among his subjects when he was away on campaign. Sigismondo de Malatesta (1417–68), who was not only a powerful condottiere but also the ruler of Rimini, was a prime example of this type of condottieri leader.

For a lesser condottiere, the rise of this system of the *casa* increased his sense of belonging. As it was organized along feudal and familial lines, loyalty to one's *casa* transcended mere material gain. For the employer this system actually introduced layers of difficulty when recruiting mercenaries and further increased the condottieri's stranglehold on military affairs. Some *case* from the same area preferred to operate in cooperation with one another, and in some regions prospective employers found it difficult to recruit condottieri as many of the local *case* shared family and political ties and would not campaign against one another. The converse also held true, and in other cases long-term feuds between condottieri *case* actually precipitated action.

For a condottiere, therefore, questions of belief and belonging were not mere abstract issues. While profit remained the overriding concern, the condottieri sought ways to engage in warfare while mentally side-stepping the strictures of the Catholic faith. Equally, individualism had no place in the mercenary profession. It was through collective action within a company or *casa* that a condottiere achieved his maximum potential.

# LIFE ON CAMPAIGN

The successful maintenance of a condottieri army on campaign represented a huge effort on the part of condottieri captains and their associated *collaterali*. In the 14th century, condottieri companies were smaller and perhaps more self-contained. By the 15th century, the more powerful Italian states were employing large armies of condottieri and these needed a considerable logistical system to function effectively.

Perhaps the most famous of all paintings depicting a condottieri subject is Paolo Uccello's *The Battle of San Romano*. Completed about 1438–40, it was composed of three panels, and these illustrated phases of the battle, which was fought in 1432. The paintings were originally commissioned by the Bartolini Salimbeni family of Florence. Lorenzo de Medici was so impressed by this series of paintings that he ordered his men forcibly to take them from the Salimbeni family. They then adorned the Medici palace, but in the 19th century they were split up and the three panels are now on display in the National Gallery, London, the Louvre in Paris and the Uffizzi in Florence. The London panel shown here is perhaps the most dramatic and shows the leader of the victorious Florentine condottieri, Niccolò Mauruzi da Tolentino, exploding into action on his grey charger, armed only with his baton of office. (National Gallery, London, Cat. 583)

During the San Romano campaign in 1432, for example, the Florentine captain-general, Niccolò da Tolentino, controlled an army of over 4,000 men. This army was of both cavalry and infantry and required large numbers of horses and baggage wagons merely to keep it mobile. When stationary it required tents for the men, firewood for fires and blacksmiths' forges in order to maintain wagons, shoe horses and service weapons. By the early 15th century, cannon were becoming more common in condottieri armies and these must have created great difficulties when on the move over roads that were very poor, while the addition of gunpowder in the supply trains introduced the risk of explosions.

By this time most armies travelled with their own surgeons and these would have required their own wagons to move their medical paraphernalia as well as tents from which to operate. A condottieri army on the move therefore required very thorough planning and administration. The French chronicler Philippe de Commynes recorded: 'As for the provision of food supplies and other things necessary for maintaining an army in the field, they do it much better than we do.'

So, even when in enemy territory, the maintenance of a condottieri army represented not only an organizational headache but also huge expense for its employers. By the 15th century, specific state officials administered an elaborate supply system for the ever-growing condottieri armies. The larger states devoted huge resources to this, employing or retaining armourers to supply their army while also collecting food and providing the transport to supply the army in the field. The richer states could actually accumulate vast reserves of arms and equipment. After the defeat of the Milanese army at Maclodio in 1427, two of the larger armourers in Milan were able to re-equip 4,000 cavalry and 2,000 infantry almost immediately.

It would appear, however, that good commissariat arrangements only carried so far. Once in enemy territory, condottieri armies had to provide their own food. This they did by foraging and pillaging as they passed through enemy territory, leaving a trail of destruction in their wake. Apart from food, the property of civilians in enemy territory was considered to be fair game and the soldiers helped themselves to portable property as well. This was a standard aspect of war and was indeed encouraged as it could force an enemy to seek some form of truce, since the alternative was to see the state and its population gradually despoiled by a ravenous army. Of course, it created great hostility to condottieri as they moved through an enemy's territory and it can only be assumed that stragglers from condottieri armies sometimes came to a brutal end at the hands of vengeful citizens.

In times of food shortage, or when the population had successfully hidden its own food, there were instances of famine-like conditions for the condottieri themselves. The sanitary arrangements that were enforced when encamped in friendly territory could also break down when on campaign, and this could lead to an outbreak of disease within the army.

A condottieri army on the move must have been an awesome sight consisting not only of cavalry, infantry and baggage wagons but also a trail of support staff including squires, smiths and surgeons, among other camp followers. It is also known that condottieri armies included women, usually prostitutes. At the battle of Brentelle in 1386, the victorious Paduan army captured 211 prostitutes in the baggage train of the defeated Venetian

army. Rather than being treated roughly, these courtesans were garlanded with flowers and joined a celebratory breakfast in Padua. It would appear that women accompanied all condottieri armies to some degree. Apart from those who came willingly, contemporary accounts also refer to condottieri abducting young women and even nuns as they passed through an enemy's territory. It seems probable that the presence of prostitutes in condottieri armies resulted in frequent outbreaks of venereal disease.

While condottieri armies preferred not to engage in long sieges, these were sometimes necessary. In 1406, for example, Pisa endured an eight-month siege by Florentine forces. Even for a well-equipped army, such long sieges must have resulted in hardship. At some stage food would have gone short, and in the Italian winter the tented accommodation must have been found wanting. Despite the best efforts of his commanders and the logistical backup provided by his employer, life on campaign for a condottiere in these circumstances must have been a miserable affair.

A mid-15th-century siege scene showing a tented camp in the field. In the background a siege-gunner is setting off a bombard. While the condottieri preferred not to expend their energies in lengthy sieges, it was sometimes necessary to do so. In the original painting, the colours of the tents and the richly caparisoned horsemen are nothing less than luxuriant. (Detail from *The Taking of Pisa* by an unknown Florentine master of the 1460s, National Gallery of Ireland, 780)

# THE CONDOTTIERE IN BATTLE

### Organization, weaponry and tactics

During the period 1300–1500, the tactics of the condottieri developed to a great degree. A condottiere of the 14th century would most probably have been a non-Italian mercenary and would have used tactics perfected through use in the Hundred Years War. The subdivision into lances mentioned earlier could consist of four to five men and included a *caporale* (the leader), his squire and a page who accompanied the lance's spare horses. These men could have further men-at-arms or archers attached to their lance.

The organization of condottieri companies varied from state to state. In Milan in the 1470s a four-man lance was the norm, while in the Papal States a five-man *corazza* was used. Five of these lances were grouped together to form a 'post', and five posts (25 lances) formed a squadron. A condottieri band (*bandiera*), often referred to as a *condotte*, numbered anywhere between 50 and 100 lances. There was room for contraction and expansion in this system of organization, and different condottieri bands, although technically the same type of unit, could vary greatly in size. This was especially true in the mid- to late 15th century, as the increasing weight of armour made more horses, and by extension more squires and pages, necessary in armies.

The age of the condottieri saw further developments in warfare. During the 15th century, light cavalry became increasingly important and were used to forage for food and, in combat, to scout and pursue a defeated enemy. By the 1470s the Italians began to recruit light cavalry known as *stradiotti*, who were usually of Greek or Albanian origin. The *stradiotti* had long served in Venetian armies but they began to be used by other Italian states. Armed with lances, bows or crossbows, they were the epitome of the light horseman. Around 1480 Naples began to employ Turkish light cavalry, who also proved to be excellent in this role.

Although condottieri warfare is usually associated with cavalry, the use of infantry also increased during the 15th century. These had previously been relegated to garrison duties as they were seen as being both vulnerable and unreliable in open actions. By the mid-15th century, condottieri armies were beginning to include large numbers of infantrymen. These were heavy infantry who wore relatively good armour

A contemporary illustration of a handgunner and artilleryman. Both wear helmets, leather jerkins and arm and leg protection. This combination provided good protection but left the gunners enough mobility to operate effectively. (Author's collection)

protection and fought with sword or pole-arm. Condottieri armies also included light infantrymen who were armed with swords and buckler shields.

While some condottieri armies utilized archers, the primary Italian projectile weapon of the 14th and 15th centuries was the crossbow. Gradually, the improvement in gunpowder technology saw these replaced by handgunners. Handguns of this period were extremely basic and easy to produce and it was also relatively easy to train men in their use. The handgunner slowly supplanted the crossbowman in the armies of the 14th and 15th centuries and not only for garrison duties but also in the field armies.

The earliest Italian handgun, the *schiopetto*, dated from the late 13th century and in its simplest form was little more than a gun barrel with a vent hole mounted on a pole. Handgunners or *schiopettieri* formed a part of most armies but some states, such as Milan, began to give them increasing prominence in their army organization. In the War of Ferrara in 1482, for example, the Milanese army had over 1,200 handgunners and just 233 crossbowmen.

The technology of handguns had also improved, making them much more effective and reliable weapons. By the late 1400s, the arquebus had been developed: a full-stocked weapon with a spring-loaded trigger. The army of the Papal States in the 1490s was capable of fielding mounted arquebusiers.

Larger gunpowder weapons proved more problematic. The technology of cannon-making advanced relatively slowly. In the field, the movement and deployment of cannon presented huge practical problems. Their slow rate of fire meant that they were often useful only for overawing less confident enemies. The usual practice was to use them in garrisons only. An increasing use of field fortifications in the 15th century meant that cannons found a new battlefield role. They were of most use in sieges and in 1357 Galeotto Malatesta was the first to use a bombard, a primitive type of mortar, in an Italian siege.

During the early 14th century the non-Italian condottieri introduced a new style of fighting. In battle the condottiere could engage his enemy on horseback using the accepted cavalry tactics of the period. However, he could also fight dismounted and two men of each lance would wield a heavy lance in a style that foreshadowed later pike tactics. This was an unusual but highly effective tactic in 14th-century Italy. A group of lances acting in this manner could come together in a large defensive hedgehog formation which opponents found difficult to break through. At the same time, if the condottieri were skilled enough they could advance in this formation in a style reminiscent of the Greek phalanxes. These tactics made condottieri companies a tough proposition on the battlefield.

The early condottieri also incorporated infantry in their companies. In the case of the English companies, these included longbowmen, who introduced a further dimension into 14th-century Italian warfare. In Italy, the crossbow was the more common projectile weapon and although

A medieval artilleryman firing a bombard, which has been aligned like a modern mortar. He is well protected with helmet, mail shirt and quilted jerkin. Developments in handguns and artillery created new areas of specialism within medieval armies which would later leave the heavily armoured cavalryman redundant. (Author's collection)

its bolt could reach a greater range and had good penetrating power, its rate of fire was much slower than that of the longbow. The longbowmen of the English companies had proved at battles such as Crécy and Poitiers that they could unleash huge deadly showers of arrows on their enemies. This gave the English companies a brief window of tactical advantage during the 14th century. In the attack, they could use their longbowmen to drive back the enemy, or even the defenders away from the walls of fortifications. In defence, the longbow was unequalled in breaking up both cavalry and infantry attacks. While improvements in crossbows and hand-held firearms would soon negate this tactical advantage, the use of the longbow by English condottiere captains brought a new and dangerous dimension to Italian warfare. While some Italian military leaders such as Alberigo da Barbiano (d. 1409) thought that the use of infantry and the dismounting of cavalry denigrated the knightly elite, such tactics gave condottiere leaders increased advantages in terms of mobility on the battlefield.

### Sforzeschi tactics

By the 15th century, two main schools of tactical thought had developed and these came to characterize condottieri battles. One of these tactical styles was developed by Muzio Attendolo (1369–1424). Born into a non-noble family in Cotignola in the Romagna region, Attendolo had served as a condottiere under Alberigo da Barbiano, himself a great condottiere and also a military theorist. It is generally accepted that Attendolo refined the tactics that he had learned as a squadron commander under Barbiano. During his career, Attendolo earned the nickname 'Sforza', which literally means 'Force'. He and his descendants would be known

A medieval clash of cavalry as depicted in Vanni's fresco of the battle of Sinalunga. The more heavily armoured cavalrymen are followed by lightly armed horsemen, presumably representing light cavalry. Note also the heraldic devices and helmet plumes of the heavy cavalry and the padded armour of their horses. (Author's photograph)

by this name and in many ways it summarized the tactical ideas of Sforza and later followers of the 'Sforzeschi' school of thought.

Like most great military leaders, Sforza inspired great loyalty from his men. He came to see this as essential to military success and through extensive training he instilled strict discipline in his condottieri. On campaign, he gathered all of his army together before a battle to ensure local superiority. He was cautious and planned each assault carefully. When he had met these self-imposed requirements, he unleashed his army in massed and carefully coordinated attacks. Unlike his mentor Barbiano, he had no reservations about using infantry and preferred to use combinations of cavalry and infantry assaults. Sforza's philosophy was simple; if commanded correctly, his attack would fall upon his enemy with the force of a massive hammer blow.

## Bracceschi tactics

The second school of tactical thought was developed by Braccio da Montone (1368–1424). Unlike Sforza, this Perugian was born into the lesser nobility but had become a condottiere to earn his living. He had also learned his profession under Barbiano and was, in his younger days, a comrade of Sforza. During his early career he had developed his own ideas on military tactics and these were a total contrast to those of Sforza and the later followers of the Sforzeschi school.

Braccio preferred to use a decisive tactical move to overwhelm his enemy and in that respect he was the master of the rapier cut rather than the hammer blow. He also inspired great loyalty among his men and trained them to a high degree. In battle his emphasis was on the tight control of his troops. He had a preference for using large cavalry formations and he committed each squadron of cavalry on a specific manoeuvre. Rather than merely unleashing his formations, he controlled them tightly, using them to find and exploit weak points in his enemies' armies. He also developed the concept of a reserve and kept back formations, later introducing fresh troops into battle as his enemies became gradually exhausted.

## Realities of combat

For an individual condottiere, these tactical considerations were probably quite irrelevant once battle was joined. From surviving paintings and accounts of the period it is quite obvious that condottieri battles were confused and brutal affairs, but there are also indications

*The Battle of Anghiari* by an unknown Florentine master of the 1460s. This painting is in the style of the school of Uccello and depicts the clash between the condottieri army of Milan, commanded by Niccolò Piccinino, and a combined Florentine and Venetian army under the renowned condottiere Francesco Sforza. The battle, on 29 June 1440, lasted for over four hours and resulted in the defeat of the Milanese, establishing Florence as the dominant power in Tuscany. Due to the relatively small number of casualties, it was later ridiculed by Machiavelli as a bloodless condottieri battle. The Tiber is shown dividing the field of battle, while the towns in the background include Borgo Sansepolcro, Citterna and Monterchi. (National Gallery of Ireland, Cat. 778)

The fight between the Bonacolsi and Gonzaga in the Piazza Sordello in Mantua, 1494. This painting by Domenico Morone is highly stylized and shows the clash between two Mantuan factions. The action is portrayed almost like a jousting session, yet close observation illustrates the brutality of close quarter fighting. (From Jacob Burkhardt, *The Civilization of the Renaissance*).

that discipline could be maintained among condottieri companies and that tactical plans were followed through.

It was Italian practice to use a cart-like vehicle known as a *carroccio* as both command post and mobile fire platform. This was usually bedecked with the flags of the city or state that controlled the army. It appears that some condottieri leaders retained this system and controlled their armies from a *carroccio* or even from their personal tent. It was more common, however, for condottieri leaders to be present in the field, moving from one scene of action to another in order to control their men and react to enemy attacks. How they communicated their intentions once battle had been joined remains unclear, although one must assume that junior officers carried orders to sub-units during a battle. Illustrations of the period sometimes show condottieri leaders travelling with trumpeters and these would have had a battlefield signalling function.

How then did the condottieri perform in battle? Contemporary chroniclers and modern historians remain divided on this subject. Niccolò Machiavelli, author of the political treatise *The Prince*, dismissed their battles as bloodless jousts. He went on to sum up condottieri leaders, stating that:

> They directed all their efforts to ridding themselves and their soldiers of any cause for fear or need for exertion; instead of fighting to the death in their scrimmages they took prisoners without demanding ransom. They never attacked garrison towns at night, and if they were besieged they never made a sortie; they did not bother to fortify their camps with stockades or ditches; they never campaigned in winter.

This could be dismissed as the gross exaggeration of a political writer who was opposed to the whole concept of employing mercenaries. Yet condottieri leaders were often not interested in fighting battles and campaigns to a decisive conclusion as this would merely have put them out of business. This attitude was typified in Sir John Hawkwood's alleged response to a Franciscan friar who had greeted him 'God give you peace'. Hawkwood responded 'Do you not know that I live by war and that peace would ruin me?'

Machiavelli's attitude is supported by other contemporary accounts. One Italian chronicler stated that condottieri were 'our natural enemies, and they despoil all of us; the only thought is to keep the upper hand and drain our wealth'. There are numerous accounts of inconclusive battles to confirm such statements. At the battle of Maclodio in 1427, the Venetian commander Carmagnola captured over 10,000 Milanese prisoners with few (if any) fatal casualties on either side although there was a huge loss of horses. Carmagnola further exasperated his combined Venetian and Florentine masters by soon releasing all of his prisoners without any ransom being paid.

The organization of condottieri armies in the field was also seriously lacking on occasion. An Italian chronicler stated:

> These Florentine troops are so badly organized that it disgusts me; the men-at-arms are spread out in confusion, often with the squadrons mixed up together in a way which seems to conform to no plan, and with squadrons as much as a mile apart. The soldiers are billeted all over the place without any provision for pioneers or other essential auxiliaries; there are very few infantry, about 700, of which 150 only are properly armed.

Such lax attitudes and disorganization often resulted in reverses on the battlefield. On 29 July 1364 a Pisan army under Sir John Hawkwood surprised a Florentine army at Cascina, a small hamlet on the Arno outside of Pisa. The Florentine commander, Galeotto Malatesta, was asleep and his men were unarmed and bathing in the river when the attack began. Despite the fact that the Pisans had breached the camp's defences, their attack stalled due to the fire from the Florentine crossbowmen. As the other Florentine soldiers armed themselves and counterattacked, a company of German condottieri in the Pisan army simply decided to leave the field. It was a prime example of how both disorganization and the cynical attitude of condottieri could combine to turn the prospect of victory into certain defeat.

Condottieri armies should not be dismissed on the basis of negative accounts of battlefield reverses, however. When properly led, trained and organized they represented a formidable force on the battlefield and their continued success and dominance of the Italian military scene is satisfactory

A 14th-century illustration of archers. The method of carrying bundles of arrows at the waist is interesting. Both men are comparatively well protected, with helmets and studded leather jerkins, while the figure on the right is also armed with a sword and buckler shield. Following the Treaty of Brétigny in 1360, many English archers travelled to Italy and were engaged as condottieri. (From Men-At-Arms 113: *The Armies of Agincourt*)

evidence of this. Further investigation of accounts of Italian battles also indicate that the idea of their being 'bloodless' was often a fiction.

The vast casualties that resulted from the battle of Parabiago in 1340 confirm this, and the fact that it was fought with snow on the ground also refutes the idea that condottieri were averse to campaigning in bad conditions. This battle resulted from the action of Lodrisio Visconti, an exiled member of the family of the rulers of Milan, who recruited an army of German and Swiss condottieri to help him gain the leadership of his native city. He gathered an army of around 2,500 cavalry and 1,000 infantry and marched on Milan. Commanded by Werner of Ürslingen and Conrad of Landau, this army of condottieri called themselves the Company of St George, the first of several condottieri bands to bear that title. Lodrisio was opposed by his cousins, Azzo and Lucchino Visconti, who called out the Milanese city militia and also hired a company of around 700 Bolognese cavalry under the command of Ettore da Panigo.

The two armies manoeuvred north of Milan and in February 1340, in frozen conditions and thick snow, the Company of St George fell on the Milanese advance guard at Parabiago. This first body of Milanese troops was quickly overcome and was pursued back towards Milan. When the Company of St George met the Milanese main body a full-scale battle developed. There was little time or thought put into tactics and each side put in a series of hard-fought assaults. Lucchino Visconti was captured by the Swiss and German condottieri and was tied to a tree but the Bolognese condottieri cavalry arrived in the nick of time from Milan and turned the tables in Milan's favour. It was the turn of the Company of St George to turn and flee and Lodrisio Visconti was captured.

**A: Armoured condottiere, Italian style, early 14th century**

1

2

3

4

5

6

7

8

A

B: Condttiere recruitment, mid-15th century

C: Condottiere column on the march, late 14th century

C

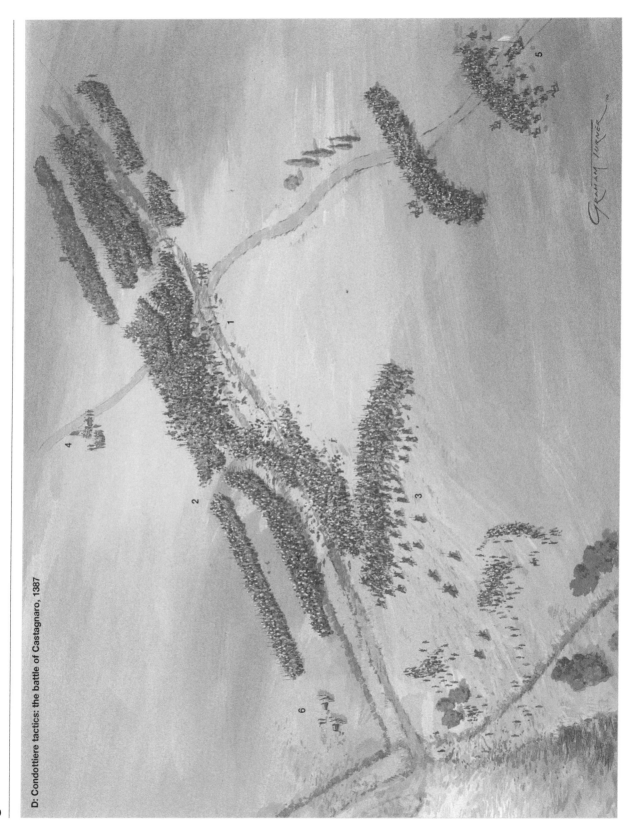

D: Condottiere tactics: the battle of Castagnaro, 1387

F

F: The battle of San Romano, 1432

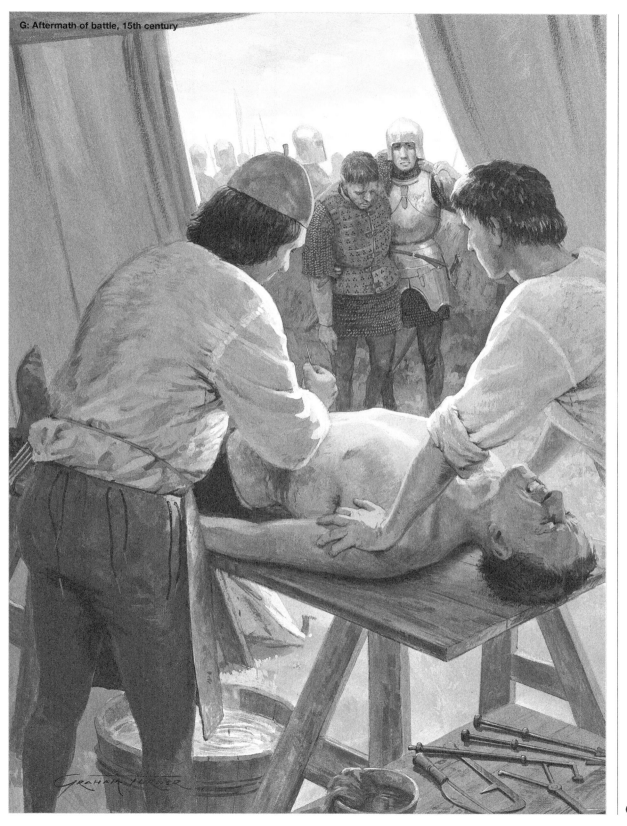

G: Aftermath of battle, 15th century

H: Armoured condottiere, late 15th century

H

A contemporary illustration of a medieval cavalry action. The majority of these horsemen wear some form of the bascinet helmet, with only a few wearing open-faced helmets. The heraldic devices are interesting, as is the variety of weapons, which include swords, axes, lances and what appears to be a war hammer being wielded in the centre of the action. (Private collection)

Over 4,000 dead from both armies lay frozen on the battlefield that night. The battle of Parabiago was typical of many early condottieri battles. It was devoid of any thought of tactics and each condottiere was expected to fling himself into the battle, despite the Arctic conditions. It was also fought to a definite conclusion, simply due to the fact that the rival Visconti factions were vying for control of Milan.

Throughout this period, the huge debate over the efficacy of the Sforzeschi and Bracceschi tactics continued to rage within the condottieri community. Some condottieri captains preferred to follow the Sforzeschi style while others preferred the Bracceschi approach. It is not surprising, given the inherent factionalism of Italian society, that these debates took on political overtones. In battle a condottiere might show a marked preference for one of these tactical styles. He might even go further and stubbornly refuse to entertain ideas outside of his own views on tactical thought. Some condottieri captains, however, displayed a remarkable agility of mind and were able to employ different types of tactic as the occasion demanded, perhaps even using elements of both tactical doctrines when deploying their troops.

The tactics employed by the Paduan commander, Sir John Hawkwood, at the battle of Castagnaro in 1387 displayed a high degree of flexibility in tactical thought (see Plate D). In this battle, Hawkwood employed tactics that could have been claimed by the adherents of either the Sforzeschi or Bracceschi schools while also using defensive tactics that he had learned during the Hundred Years War. He had been forced to call off a siege at Verona due to the small size of his army and in March 1387 was retreating towards his supply base at Castelbaldo with an army of 7,000 mounted men-at-arms, 1,000 infantry and around 600 English archers who were operating as mounted infantry. Hawkwood's army also had a small artillery train that consisted of a few bombards. He was pursued by a Veronese army commanded by Giovanni de Ordelaffi which consisted of over 9,000 mounted men-at-arms, 2,600 infantry (both crossbowmen and pikemen) and also an unspecified number of militia. Apart from outnumbering Hawkwood's force, the Veronese army also had a larger artillery train consisting of over 20 bombards and

A detail of Vanni's fresco of the battle of Sinalunga in 1363 in the Palazzo Pubblico in Siena. The confusion and horror of a medieval cavalry mêlée are obvious, while towards the bottom of the fresco the dead seem already to have been stripped of their armour and their wounds can be seen. For condottieri of this period, the majority of serious battlefield wounds were fatal. (Author's photograph)

ribaulds. This artillery was, however, straggling far behind the main Veronese army and would play no part in the battle.

Faced with such a large force, Hawkwood would have been excused for falling back on Castelbaldo, and indeed the Veronese were expecting to have to besiege this town. Instead he chose a very strong position north of the hamlet of Castagnaro and arrayed his army in a defensive formation that echoed those used in some of the great battles of the Hundred Years War. He drew up his army in two lines of dismounted men-at-arms, supported by his cavalry and mounted archers. To the right of his line he placed his few pieces of artillery. To the front, his army was protected by a deep drainage ditch, which also tapered around to the left of the Paduan position. Also on his left, the ground was marshy and prevented an enemy cavalry charge. Hawkwood's right flank was protected by the Alveo Canal and farther to his right was the Adige river. Due to recent heavy rainfall, the ground was damp and soft and seemingly unsuited for large-scale cavalry action.

The Veronese attack developed around noon on 11 March 1387. Ordelaffi had similarly positioned his infantry and dismounted men-at-arms in two lines which were supported by cavalry to their rear. Farther back still, he held his militia and also a group of cavalry to protect the Veronese *carroccio*. He had set his men to making fascines which were to be used to cross the drainage ditch that separated his army from the Paduans. The main effort of the Veronese assault fell on the centre of Hawkwood's line and, as the Veronese filled certain areas of the ditch with fascines and crossed it, the second lines of both armies were committed to the assault. Ordelaffi, judging that flanking attacks around either end of the Paduan line were not possible, now committed all of his infantry and some of his militia to this central attack. An intense, Sforzeschi-style, contest developed and it seemed likely that the battle would be won by the side that could bring the largest number of men to bear in an assault on the centre of the battle front. As the Veronese pressed their advantage in numbers home, they managed to cross the ditch to the Paduan front.

Hawkwood, however, had other ideas on how to win this battle. He had reconnoitred to the north-east of his own position and had discovered that it was possible to lead cavalry through the river shallows and ditches and from there attack the left rear of the Veronese line. In the Bracceschi style, he led his mounted archers and men-at-arms in a sweeping flanking movement that was to prove to be the decisive manoeuvre. He also brought his Paduan crossbowmen and when this force reached the Veronese side of both the drainage ditch and the Alveo Canal, they fell on the rear of their enemies' positions. The archers and crossbowmen showered the Veronese formation before Hawkwood's cavalry attacked. Confusion reigned in the Veronese lines as, fully engaged to their front, they were now attacked from the rear. An attempted counter-attack was beaten off and Hawkwood is reported to have flung his commander's baton into the mêlée, promising a reward to the soldier who ventured into the midst of the Veronese to retrieve it. As the Veronese broke and fled they further impeded Ordelaffi who was bringing up his own cavalry reserve to counter-attack.

The final initiative now rested with the Paduans and Hawkwood led his men forward to seize the Veronese *carroccio* and force a surrender. All of the Veronese condottieri leaders were taken prisoner and also a further 4,600 men-at-arms and around 800 infantry. One Veronese detachment, commanded by Giovanni da Isola, refused to surrender and was slaughtered to a man. Total casualties numbered over 700 dead and 800 wounded.

While contemporary chroniclers denigrated the condottieri for the supposedly lukewarm manner in which they engaged in warfare, Castagnaro was a decisive victory and was one of several during this period. It was a battle in which different types of troops and tactics were used. It was also a hard-fought action in which some condottieri were taken prisoner while others continued to resist and were killed. Ultimately, it was a prime example of the abilities and potential of condottieri captains and their armies.

For a condottiere, such set-piece battles held all the inherent dangers of the medieval battlefield. Those who fought dismounted as infantrymen, archers or crossbowmen had to confront their opposite numbers in an often confused skirmish. They faced further dangers from projectile weapons which now included not only arrows and crossbow bolts, but also the bullets and balls from handguns and cannon. Perhaps the ultimate fear of all infantry was to be outflanked and charged by enemy cavalry; to face a humiliating death as their formation was broken and they were run down by armoured horsemen.

For a mounted condottiere, life was equally hazardous. Contemporary illustrations depict clashes of cavalry as confusing and bloody affairs, the shock of the impact apparent as riders are unhorsed and ridden over. They could find their charges broken or stopped by the projectiles fired at them by archers, crossbowmen and handgunners. There was also the fear of being unhorsed by infantry and facing an ignominious death on the ground as the enemy soldiers searched for chinks in suits of armour through which to dispatch prostrate knights. How many expensively armoured condottieri were killed by the thrust of a cheap dagger through the visor of their helmet?

The Italian climate itself presented further dangers for a condottiere. Campaigns were usually carried out in the summer months and in intense heat. Contemporary accounts refer to the hardships endured by armoured men in such a climate. One account stated that at the battle of San Romano in 1432, several condottieri expired in the heat of early summer, literally being cooked alive in their armour. At the battle of San Egideo in 1416, the Perugian army under Carlo Malatesta disintegrated as his men left their positions on the battlefield in order to slake their thirst in the Tiber river, defeated by the heat and dust of an Italian July as much as by the tactics of his enemy, Braccio da Montone.

## Sieges

While sieges were relatively common in medieval warfare, in general condottieri leaders preferred not to engage in them. The strong defences

*The Taking of Pisa* by an unknown Florentine master of the 1460s. This painting, also in the style of the school of Uccello, shows scenes from the eight-month siege of Pisa by a Florentine army in 1406. At the end of the siege, the victorious Florentine army entered Pisa carrying loaves of bread impaled on their lances as a conciliatory gesture; this is depicted here. (National Gallery of Ireland, Cat. 780)

of many Italian towns meant that they were long, dangerous and costly affairs that required a lot of siege equipment. Instead, a condottiere captain would prefer to drive his enemy back within the safety of his town walls and then begin despoiling the surrounding countryside while his enemy looked on. Crops were destroyed or, if transport was available, were harvested. Livestock was taken or killed. Vines were cut down and wells poisoned. It was common for houses to have been built beneath a city's walls and, as the inhabitants sheltered within the defences, the condottieri would loot and burn their houses. This process of spoliation could not only demoralize an enemy but could, on occasion, force him to accept a peace treaty. A form of biological warfare was also employed by the condottieri, who would catapult rotting corpses into besieged towns.

Occasionally full-scale sieges were engaged in, and the condottieri developed their own style with respect to these. The medieval chronicler Jean de Bueil later wrote an unflattering description of condottieri methods for attacking a town.

> They spy out a walled castle for a day or two beforehand; then, collecting together a group of thirty or forty brigands, they approach it from one side and then from another. At the break of day they burst in and set fire to a house, making so much noise that the inhabitants think that there must be a thousand men-at-arms among them and flee in all directions. Then they break into the houses and loot them before departing loaded with spoil.

Even the difficult business of a medieval siege was not pursued without profit in mind. Of course, extortion of various forms was a major weapon in the condottieri's arsenal. A powerful condottiere could demand payments for various reasons: controlling his men, lifting a siege, returning looted Church property. In 1416, Braccio da Montone sold Bologna back to its own citizens for the price of 82,000 florins. No personage, regardless of how august he might be, was exempt from such practices. In 1376 Sir John Hawkwood kidnapped a cardinal in the hope of getting his employer, Pope Gregory XI, to pay him arrears in his pay.

### Devastation, prisoners and massacres
Apart from devastating the area surrounding a besieged city, the condottieri would despoil enemy territory as they passed through it. For

A detail from Lippo Vanni's fresco in the Palazzo Pubblico in Siena. It depicts the battle of Sinalunga in 1363, in which the forces of Siena routed the English Compagnia del Cappello, a company of freebooters that was ravaging the locality. Preceded by trumpeters, the Sienese captain (presumably Giordano Orsini) leads his men into battle. His leg armour is interesting and suggests that studded leather cuisses are being worn over mail leggings. He also appears to be wielding some form of baton of office rather than a sword. (Author's photograph)

this a condottiere would usually employ peasants, who would then prosecute his 'scorched earth' policy. The peasant bands that carried out such work were referred to as *quastatori* or 'devastators'. If in turn the *quastatori* were captured by the enemy, or even by the locals whose territory they had despoiled, they could expect a grisly end.

Against such a backdrop of brutality and spoliation, one would expect that prisoners would be treated harshly, but this was rarely the case. Captured condottieri were, after all, merely unfortunate members of the same profession. A certain professional courtesy was observed and captured condottieri leaders were usually freed on the payment of a ransom. Condottieri leaders were also disinclined to keep lesser soldiers captive as feeding and billeting them would require considerable expense. It was normal for ordinary soldiers to be merely disarmed and sent on their way. The mutilation of captured troops, especially archers, was not as common as it had been during the Hundred Years War.

Such leniency was not extended to the wider population. From contemporary descriptions, it is obvious that many condottieri held the population as a whole in general contempt. As a result of this attitude, civilians were often the victims in the midst of the collateral damage of medieval warfare. There were also instances where civilians were deliberately singled out and made the object of atrocities. Contemporary accounts make frequent references to such events, and while a certain

A 15th-century illustration of mercenaries burning and pillaging a village. Although this illustration actually depicts an incident in the Hussite wars, similar practices were employed by condottieri, and such treatment of civilians in enemy territory was seen as a standard feature of warfare. (Author's collection)

critical faculty must be employed with respect to these sources, nevertheless in some cases the claims about an atrocity are corroborated by several accounts. For example, there can be little doubt that a detestable atrocity took place at Cesena in 1377.

The town of Cesena was one of the few remaining strongholds of Papal authority in the Romagna region in 1377. It was controlled by Robert of Geneva, who had been appointed as cardinal legate in the town. To endorse his overlordship of the town, Robert commanded a garrison of Breton condottieri and also had English and Italian condottieri at his disposal. Severe food shortages in the winter of 1376–77 led to a series of confrontations between the townspeople and the Breton condottieri, and one of these incidents resulted in the death of several of the cardinal's men. His initial actions were conciliatory but in secret he planned revenge on the people of Cesena for this affront to his authority.

English condottieri under Hawkwood and Italian condottieri under Alberigo da Barbiano were summoned to the town to support Robert's Bretons. Late in the night of 2 February 1377, these condottieri swarmed through the gates of the town and began a massacre of reprisal. Men, women and children were cut down without mercy. No-one was spared and even the men and women of Cesena's religious community were among the casualties. Fires were started deliberately and whole areas of the town were destroyed. The condottieri gave themselves over to an orgy of murder, rape and looting and those who tried to flee were either cut down at the gates of the town or drowned while trying to cross the water-filled moat.

Even if one believes only a fraction of the surviving accounts, a horrific picture of the 'rape of Cesena' emerges. It was later stated that the town squares of Cesena were piled high with bodies and one account records that a child hiding in the church of San Antonio nel Campo Baorio was murdered and left on the altar. Those not immediately murdered were held prisoner and tortured so as to reveal the location of hidden money. Others were taken prisoner and ransom was demanded from their families. Hundreds of women were carried off as spoil and never seen again. The records of the town were taken out and burned, the history of Cesena up to 1377 quite simply being erased. Estimates of the dead range from 3,000 to 8,000 people. In 1378, on the death of Pope Gregory, Robert of Geneva was declared to be the new pope by one of the factions of cardinals. As Clement VII, the 'butcher of Cesena' began a line of 'anti-Popes' and precipitated a schism that was to last for over 40 years.

For a condottiere, experience of battle could encompass many things. Warfare could involve the deployment of armies of various sizes and the use of different tactics and weapons on the field. It held all the inherent dangers of medieval warfare, coupled with the particular difficulty of campaigning in the hot Italian climate. A condottiere might also use various tactics of intimidation, extortion and spoliation to overwhelm his enemy. On occasion, the methods of the condottieri could acquire bestial connotations as the civilian population were subjected to atrocities of Biblical proportions.

**This 14th-century illustration of the siege of Melun indicates the level of duplicity seen in medieval warfare. The besieging leader parleys with his enemies to the left of the image; his sappers are shown undermining the city walls to the right. While this depiction is of the Norman knight Bertrand Du Guesclin (1320–80), such methods would have been used by the condottieri. (Private collection)**

# CONSPIRACY AND BETRAYAL

The Italian states that employed condottieri faced, of course, the perennial problem of dealing with mercenaries. What if their enemies secretly paid their condottieri to betray them in battle? Despite the formal and rigid nature of the *condotte* that the mercenaries signed, many condottieri showed no scruples when it came to taking payment from a supposed enemy in order to betray their employers. There are numerous instances of such betrayals in the histories of the period and there seem to have been as many ways for a condottiere to betray his employers as there were for him to serve them.

During the war between Pisa and Florence in 1364, the Pisan commanders, who included Sir John Hawkwood, Annechin Bongarden and Albert Sterz, led an army of over 12,000 English, Swiss and German condottieri. The opening phase of their campaign was highly successful and they drove the Florentine army back within the gates of the city. The Pisan army found itself commanding the city from its camps on the heights of Fiesole and Montughi and, although they did not have the forces or equipment to engage in a full siege, they could contain the Florentine troops within the city walls and then ravage the countryside around.

The Florentines, however, judged the quality of the Pisan army and its commanders well, and decided to dissipate the surrounding army through wholesale bribery. In total, it is estimated that the Florentines spent over 100,000 gold florins in bribes and the Pisan commanders agreed initially to a five-month truce and then to lift the siege altogether. To his credit, Hawkwood refused both the bribes and the offer of a new contract in Florentine service. Those who had refused Florentine advances now numbered around 800 men and they had to withdraw to Pisa; the Florentine army was able to follow on their trail, carrying out reprisals up to the gates of the city. The collapse of the Pisan position of advantage in 1364 remains a prime example of how the condottieri's susceptibility to bribery could change the outcome of a campaign.

It was not only during sieges that such tactics of betrayal were employed. There were cases of condottieri secretly meeting emissaries of the enemy beforehand to arrange the outcome of future battles. In 1386 the forces of Padua and Venice clashed in the battle of Brentelle. The Doge of Venice, Antonio Vernier, had hoped that the battle would bring a decisive victory, but his condottieri troops had been bribed beforehand and retreated at the critical moment, leaving the field to the Paduans.

In dealing with this type of treachery, the employers of condottieri were at a considerable disadvantage. The fact that they employed condottieri often meant that they had no military forces of their own. They were not totally powerless, however, and occasionally could take their revenge on a condottiere who had displeased or betrayed them. Perhaps the most notable example of this was the vengeance taken on the condottiere known as Carmagnola (Francesco Bussone). Born the humble son of a shepherd, Carmagnola had become one of Italy's leading condottieri and served Milan before being employed in the Venetian service. Recognized as a great tactical commander, he had led his army to victory over the Milanese at Maclodio in 1427, but during the war between Venice and Milan that simmered throughout the 1420s and 1430s, his behaviour came to be seen as suspect by the Venetian 'Council f Ten'. It became increasingly obvious that he was playing them off against his old employer, Milan. During the campaign of 1431–32, he made a series of decisions that affected the Venetian position badly and his employers recognized that this represented treachery rather than mere incompetence. His decisions resulted in Venetian reverses at Lodi, Soncino and Cremona and he was summoned to Venice to account for his actions.

Perhaps surprisingly Carmagnola actually answered this summons and was arrested on his arrival. On the third day of his interrogation, torture was applied by a 'master torturer from Padua'. His feet were burned and his arm broken and he confessed to his secret dealings with Milan. At his trial he was found guilty and was sentenced to death. On 5 May 1432 he was led, bound and gagged, to the traditional Venetian place of execution: 'between the lion and St Theodore'. It took three blows of the axe to sever his head. However, while condottieri were often criticized for their mercenary and occasionally treacherous behaviour, the record of their employers was often worse. The officials of Venice had the worst reputation for such treachery and were a byword for double-dealing. At different times they tried to poison both Francesco Sforza and Filippo Maria Visconti. It was perhaps Cesare Borgia, however, who represented the ultimate example of a dangerous employer. On one occasion he summoned three of his condottieri captains to his castle for a meeting only to have them strangled when they arrived.

This climate of betrayal meant that condottieri were often used as tools in other conspiracies that took place away from the battlefield. During this period, political assassination was common. In December 1476, for example, Duke Galeazzo Maria Sforza, a son of Francesco Sforza but also a notorious tyrant, was assassinated while at mass at the church of Santo Stefano in Milan. Murderous conspiracies were common and any condottiere might find himself being approached by some faction that wanted to liquidate its political rivals.

## The Pazzi plot

One of the notorious conspiracies of the 15th century was the Pazzi plot of 1478. The members of the Pazzi family were some of the most vocal and violent opponents to the rule of Lorenzo de Medici in Florence. The Pazzis and their supporters obtained the tacit sanction of Pope Sixtus IV and also the support of the archbishop of Pisa, Francesco Salviati. They and their supporters planned to kill Lorenzo, his brother Giuliamo de Medici and other Medici supporters in a surprise attack. Their tool in this plot was Gian Battista de Montesecco, a noted condottiere who led a company of Perugian condottieri. From Montesecco's own confession, it would appear that he joined the plot with some reluctance and had warned the conspirators, 'My lords, beware of what you do. Florence is a big affair'. He finally agreed to aid the plot, on condition that he was not asked to act against Lorenzo de Medici personally. Ultimately, these qualms proved to be his undoing, as it is arguable that the plot would have been a success had he dealt with Medici himself.

The plot was sprung on 26 April 1478, while Lorenzo and Giuliamo de Medici were at mass in the Duomo in Florence. Montesecco and his men seized the Santa Croce gate while an ambush was sprung for

Lorenzo in the cathedral. At the moment of consecration, four assassins struck. Francesco de Pazzi and Bernardo Bandini Baroncelli (a sometime condottiere) attacked and killed Giuliamo de Medici, Pazzi being so overcome with his own fury that he stabbed himself in the thigh. Lorenzo's would-be assassins were two disgruntled priests, and when they botched their attempt he managed to escape.

Archbishop Salviati led some of the Perugian condottieri to the Palazzo della Signoria with the intention of seizing the seat of civic power. The condottieri were led into a room with concealed catches on the doors and were trapped while the archbishop was clubbed to the ground and captured. Lorenzo's revenge was swift and brutal: the trapped condottieri were butchered by Medici supporters while the leading conspirators were tortured and executed. The two failed priest-assassins were castrated and hanged. Francesco de Pazzi and Archbishop Salviati were hanged from the windows of the Palazzo della Signoria, the archbishop biting Pazzi as he struggled at the end of his rope. Other members of the Pazzi family were also executed. Montesecco, the reluctant condottiere conspirator, provided a confession, presumably under torture, and was beheaded in the Bargello. His confession survives in the Florence archives and is the main source on this failed conspiracy.

### Conspiracies against condottiere

While condottieri frequently became embroiled in such political conspiracies, they were also occasionally the target of similar plots. The noted condottiere Biordo Michelotti had returned to his native Perugia in 1393 and had soon established himself as overlord of the city. The city's politically divided population had been at each other's throats for more than a decade and this had resulted in numerous assassinations and massacres. Michelotti restored a level of peace and normality but this was resented by Pope Boniface IX, who had tried to arbitrate in the Perugian disputes but had failed miserably. The level of Papal involvement in the Michelotti conspiracy is still debated but it should be noted that the ringleader was Abbott Guidalotti, who had previously been the Pope's host when he was staying in Perugia and was recognized to be Boniface's spokesman in the city.

On a Sunday morning in March 1398, the abbot led his followers to Michelotti's house, choosing this moment as he knew that the majority of the city's population would be at mass. Announcing that he had important news for Michelotti, the abbot and his party gained admittance to the condottiere's house. The signal for the attack to be sprung was to be the abbot's kiss of greeting. When the unsuspecting Michelotti arrived he was duly betrayed with this Judas kiss and hacked and stabbed to the ground, it later being reported that the floor of his house ran red with blood. As an extra precaution, the assassins used poisoned daggers, although the attack was so violent that these proved unnecessary. The reaction of Michelotti's followers was equally savage. Although the murderous abbot managed to escape, his family home was burned to the ground, his aged father dying in the fire. Without Michelotti's leadership, the city was soon hopelessly divided once again.

For a condottiere, therefore, numerous other dangers existed off the battlefield. He could find himself being drawn into a conspiracy which, if badly executed, would result in his own grisly demise. In a similar way, a condottiere who rose to a position of power could find himself the target of an assassination plot, while in general employers could simply never be totally trusted.

# AFTERMATH OF BATTLE

### Medical treatment

What were the chances for a condottiere who had been wounded in battle? For even moderately serious wounds, the prognosis was not good. Western medicine during this period was simply light-years behind its Eastern counterpart and surgical practices were primitive in the extreme. Many fundamental anatomical lessons had yet to be learned, while certain aspects of medical knowledge, such as methods for trepanning the skull, had been effectively forgotten in Western medicine. There had, of course, been universities in Italy since the 12th century, the University of Bologna being one of the first to be founded in Europe, and there were several seats of medical learning in Italy; but medical practice and anatomical experimentation were greatly hampered by the influence of the Catholic Church, which frowned on the dismemberment of corpses. There was, therefore, limited

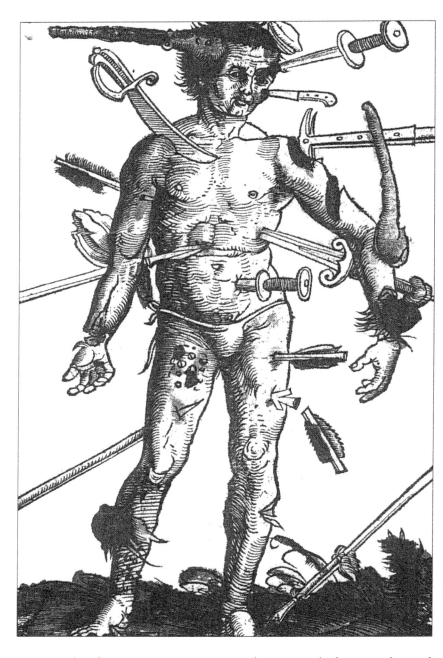

A 'wound man' from Hans Gersdorff's *Feldtbuch der Wundarztney* (1517). Although this was intended as a reference guide for surgeons in the treatment of battlefield wounds, many of the injuries depicted here were beyond the scope of medieval doctors.

opportunity for surgeons to engage in anatomical research, and medical knowledge stagnated as a result.

Another problem was that, while the universities produced a certain number of physicians and surgeons, there were not enough to meet the demands of either the civilian or the military population. If lucky, a wounded condottiere might find himself treated by a university-trained surgeon. If not, he might fall into the hands of one of the numerous self-trained surgeons and upgraded apothecaries whose treatments were often dangerously amateurish and experimental. It is little wonder that Petrarch commented, 'There is no quicker way to health than to do without a doctor.'

A medieval anatomy lesson. Many of the universities of medieval Italy had chairs of anatomy but the Catholic Church discouraged widespread dissection of corpses. Medical knowledge stagnated as a result and any wounded condottiere faced a grim prospect. (From Burkhardt, *The Civilization of the Renaissance in Italy*)

There were certain wounds that could be treated on the battlefield. Breaks to the arms and legs could be splinted and some cuts, even quite deep ones, could be sutured. Illustrations of surgeons' instruments (tools might be a better word) also show different types of cauterizing irons and the cauterization of open wounds appears to have been commonplace. Contemporary illustrations of surgeons operating often include a depiction of some kind of brazier that could be used for heating cauterizing irons. Some surgeons would even attempt to suture severed nerves and there was also a range of treatments for a whole series of general ailments including ulcers, cataracts and bladder stones (see Plate G).

Serious battlefield injuries were, however, untreatable and spelled certain death for any unlucky condottiere. Among the most dangerous were wounds inflicted by arrows or crossbow bolts. A barbed or 'bearded' arrow was extremely difficult to extract without causing further injury. Standard treatments for this kind of wound were to burn the arrow out or pour boiling oil into the wound, both of which were extremely harmful.

Heavy blows from swords could also result in complicated wounds and often drove pieces of mail, armour or cloth into the injury, causing infection. A puncture wound to the stomach would inevitably lead to peritonitis, for which there was no cure at this time. Equally, puncture wounds to the lungs would result in death. Wounds to the head were untreatable and any depressed fractures of the skull were fatal. The method of diagnosing such wounds was to stopper the patient's ears, nose and mouth and then make him blow. If air then hissed through the skull, it was obviously fractured and untreatable. In the same way, wounds of the throat that hissed air were also considered to be impossible to treat. The standard procedure in these cases was to leave the patient alone to die.

The outlook was not good, therefore, for wounded condottieri. The terms of many *condotte* refer to an obligation on the part of the employer to provide some recourse to medical treatment. While billeted near towns, condottieri could make use of the local surgeons. In the field this was more problematic, but contemporary illustrations show surgeons working from their tents in military camps, so it would appear that large armies travelled with their own surgeon or surgeons. A wounded condottiere could reasonably hope to be carried from the field by his friends to the tent or lodging of the nearest surgeon. The skill of that surgeon was very much a matter of chance.

On a more positive level, there were considerable medical advances during this period and, although treatments might seem primitive by modern standards, there was some level of progress. In the late 1400s, a wounded condottiere had a better chance of effective treatment than his predecessors had possessed in the early 14th century. Europe was ravaged by plague – the Black Death – between 1347 and 1350, and the panic that this epidemic created resulted in a resurgence of medical experimentation and theorizing. Numerous medical texts were produced on treating the plague and other ailments.

From the 15th century, a recurring motif in these medical texts was the 'wound man', which was intended to illustrate various types of combat wound with suggestions for their treatment in the text. Ironically, while badly wounded condottieri might not expect effective treatment, emergency battlefield interventions allowed surgeons to engage in hands-on anatomical study. This was another factor that led to an improvement of medical knowledge during this period. In general, however, the chances of effective medical intervention for any wounded condottiere were not good. Accounts of condottieri battles sometimes refer to the survivors dispatching wounded men on the battlefield. Considering the limited medical options available, this could well be construed as an act of mercy rather than one of brutality.

**Rewards**

The immediate and obvious reward for any condottiere was obviously monetary. This was reflected in the complexity of their *condotte* and the systems of payment that these contracts entailed. A condottiere could also enrich himself through his campaigns as he was allowed to keep any portable property that he looted from the enemy, including horses, livestock and farm equipment.

Some condottieri aspired to greater things and during the 15th century many requested and received rights of citizenship from the states that employed them. Having attained this level of respectability, such condottieri could later rise to positions of authority in the state's administration. From the late 15th century onwards, an increasing number of Italians became condottieri and many of these came from the lesser nobility or even more humble backgrounds. For some of these condottieri, what they sought was a position of power and responsibility in their home town or region. Such ambitions can be seen in the efforts of Braccio da Montone to gain control of his home town of Perugia.

Other condottieri were rulers of towns and small princedoms in their own right. The condottiere Francesco Carrara (d. 1393) controlled the city of Padua, and his descendants retained control of the city for nearly a century. The members of the Este family controlled Ferrara while the Malatestas were lords of Rimini. For such Italian grandees, the career of a condottiere allowed them to gain the wealth that would maintain them in their positions of power. It also held the second attraction of allowing them on occasion to wage war on their enemies.

For some condottieri, their rise to positions of power was nothing short of meteoric. The most obvious example of this was the rise to power of the Sforza family. This dynasty was founded by Muzio Attendolo (1369–1424), later known as Sforza, who was born into relative poverty and remained illiterate for the whole of his life. Despite these shortcomings, he became one of the most successful and powerful condottieri in Italy. His son, Francesco Sforza (1401–66), continued in the family profession, and, through his skill as a condottiere and a fortuitous marriage into the Visconti family, became duke of Milan in 1450. Within the space of two generations, the Sforza family had risen from humble origins to the lordship of one of the most powerful city states in Italy.

Detail of Donatello's equestrian monument to Gattamelata, the 'honeyed cat'. This condottiere's real name was Erasmo da Narni and he was born the son of an Umbrian baker. By the end of his career, the skilled condottiere had risen to the ranks of the Venetian nobility. This statue in the Piazza del Santo in Padua was the first equestrian statue to be cast since classical times. (Author's photograph)

# CONCLUSION

The 1520s saw the resumption of the war between the Holy Roman Emperor, Charles V, and the French king, Francis I. The conflict between these two rulers was played out in northern Italy and, due to an alliance between Francis and Pope Clement VII, the French troops and Italian condottieri fought as allies and clashed with the Imperial army in a series of battles such as at Pavia in 1525.

In the bitterly cold winter of 1526, there was a series of skirmishes between Imperial Landsknechts and Italian troops along the banks of the Mincio River. During one of these an Italian captain-general was hit in the thigh by a cannon ball. He was Giovanni delle Bande Neri, son of a Medici father and a Sforza mother. Known as 'Giovanni of the Black Band' due to the mourning he and his men had worn on the death of Pope Leo in 1521, he had also been known as 'the Invincible' by his allies and 'the Great Devil' by his enemies. The survivor of numerous battles and skirmishes, Giovanni was carried to Mantua, where it was later reported that he held a candle for the surgeon as his leg was amputated. Gangrene set in and he died a few days later. He was the last of the great condottieri leaders.

In truth, the position of the condottieri was being constantly eroded in the final decades of the 1400s. The French invasion of Italy in 1494 is often seen as the death-knell of the condottieri. In the face of a large, unified and almost national army, the resistance of the condottieri proved ineffective. This was again the case following the resumption of war in 1521, a phase of conflict that would eventually lead to the Sack of Rome in 1527. Yet, one could argue that it was not the condottieri system that was at fault. It was the political factionalism of Italy and the lack of political determination to resist both French and Imperial incursions that resulted in military defeat.

In practical terms, the organization and greater size of French, Imperial and later Spanish armies also meant that the deployment of relatively small armies of condottieri was not sufficient to oppose them on the battlefield. The late 1400s and early 1500s saw an increasing use of gunpowder weapons and, as hand-held weapons became more effective, the use of armoured cavalry and dismounted men-at-arms looked more and more redundant. Despite the fact that the condottieri were highly trained, experienced and well equipped, they were becoming increasingly ineffective against armies that used ever-greater numbers of firearms. It was not ironic that the condottieri were superseded by armies whose men were trained and equipped much more cheaply than they themselves had been. The rise in what we would recognize as standing armies spelled the end of the free-lance condottiere.

To dismiss the condottieri as mere mercenaries would be a gross oversimplification. Their relationship with their employers and the inter-relationship between different leaders and their companies were extremely complex. In terms of equipment and tactics, their style of warfare was constantly evolving. The historiography of the condottieri has been overwhelmingly negative and this is because it was largely informed by contemporary writers such as Machiavelli who detested the condottieri, their style of warfare and the extortion they practised. Ultimately one could argue that the condottieri merely responded to the needs of a society that was fundamentally divided. The leaders and general public of the various Italian states were content to employ condottieri to prosecute their many wars so that they in turn could engage in commerce and factional politics. It seems somewhat petty that Italian writers should later complain about the methods of the condottieri when one considers that Italian society had essentially ceded military power to them.

Much has been made of condottieri excesses, and the Cesena massacre stands as a prime example. It could be pointed out that such atrocities were perpetuated not on the orders of condottieri captains but rather by political leaders. Such atrocities were commonplace across Europe, and compared with some of the acts carried out by other kings and princes the condottieri could appear as positively benevolent. Indeed the ranks of the condottieri contained extremely educated and cultured figures such as Francesco Sforza and Federigo da Montefeltro, dedicated humanists who acted as patrons of the arts. Compared to the lives of some their contemporaries, such as the Borgias, it could be argued that some condottieri leaders were almost paragons of virtue.

The bad press received by the condottieri arose because the members of their profession enjoyed a military monopoly on the Italian peninsula. For a condottiere, his supreme loyalty was to the members of his band or *casa*. On a wider level, his loyalty was to the profession itself. It was in his interest to prolong wars, as through the absence of decisive victory the condottieri profession was self-perpetuating. The men of the condottieri profession effectively held the Italian peninsula to ransom for the best part of 200 years. The intervention of large foreign armies, which were superior in arms and organization, ultimately ended the indecisiveness of Italian warfare and the condottieri system.

A close-up of Verrocchio's equestrian monument to Bartolomeo Colleoni in Venice. Although commissioned after Colleoni's death in 1475, it captures the commanding presence of this powerful condottiere who served both Milan and Venice. (Author's photograph)

Andrea del Verrocchio's equestrian monument to Bartolomeo Colleoni in the Campo SS Giovanni e Paolo in Venice. Commissioned about 1479, it is perhaps the most impressive public monument ever created to commemorate any condottiere. Colleoni was one of the most successful condottieri leaders of his era, yet probably few of the thousands of tourists who wander past his monument every year realize that he was once one of the most powerful men in Italy. (Author's photograph)

Yet echoes of the condottieri remain. While the great condottieri battles are seldom remembered, modern travellers in Italy can see relics of numerous condottieri all around them if they choose to look closely enough. These range from huge public monuments such as Verrocchio's imposing statue of Bartolomeo Colleoni in Venice to the elaborate tomb of Sigismondo de Malatesta in Rimini. The condottieri were also the subjects of paintings by numerous artists including Titian and Uccello, and these can be found in galleries across Europe. It was often fashionable for powerful condottieri to be memorialized with commemorative medals; and examples of these can be found in numerous collections and are often forgotten, neglected and not even on display. In literature, the condottieri have remained a topic of fascination, and they have appeared in the works of writers such as Sir Walter Scott, Ann Radcliffe and Sir Arthur Conan Doyle.

In the centuries that have passed since the demise of the condottieri system, mercenaries have continued to be employed in warfare. Various armies have used regiments and legions of Germans, Swiss, Austrians and mercenaries of other nationalities. Widespread migration and emigration in the 19th century resulted in men of numerous nationalities serving in the armies of the American Civil War, while other 'foreigners' served in European armies. Their enemies have often criticized them as being mere mercenaries. None of them experienced the same level of power and autonomy that was enjoyed by the condottieri. The age of the mercenary controlling a military monopoly has passed.

Since the coalition invasion of Iraq in 2003, hundreds of private contractors have flocked to that country and are at the time of writing employed carrying out different types of duties. Although highly paid,

Bartolomeo Colleoni in a more humble pose as he appears in the anonymous 15th-century fresco known as *Crucifixion with Colleoni* in the Casa Colleoni in Bergamo. Although somewhat worn looking, this fresco does show some details of his suit of plate armour. (Author's photograph).

The last of the condottieri: Giovanni de Medici, more commonly known as 'Giovanni delle Bande Neri'. The son of Caterina Sforza and a descendant of Cosimo de Medici, Giovanni was the only member of the Medici family to become a condottiere and is generally acknowledged to have been the last great leader of condottieri. This monument by Bandinelli was completed about 1540 and is in the Piazza San Lorenzo in Florence. (Author's photograph)

this is extremely dangerous work and there have been a number of casualties. The majority are ex-soldiers and the companies that employ them insist that they are not mercenaries but rather 'contractors'. It is perhaps not surprising that some members of the media have noticed the analogy that the use of this term suggests and several sources have referred to these men as 'modern condottieri'.

## MUSEUMS, COLLECTIONS AND RE-ENACTMENT

Since the 18th century, travellers to Italy undertaking the 'grand tour' have bought and collected pieces of Italian armour. As a result, there are 14th- and 15th-century Italian weapons and armour in private and public collections across the world.

In England, the Royal Armouries at Leeds has a large collection of Italian medieval armour and this includes armour for both mounted and dismounted combat. The Art Gallery and Museum at Kelvingrove in Glasgow possesses an exquisite suit of 15th-century armour known as the 'Avant Armour' and there is further material of relevance in the Wallace Collection in London. On the continent, there are numerous Italian pieces in the vast collection of armour held at the Musée de l'Armée (Les Invalides) in Paris. A full listing of museums that contain Italian armour of this period would be unfeasible in a book of this length, but further items can be found in the collections at the Palace of the Grand Masters in Valetta, the Stibbert Museum in Florence,

Churburg Castle in the Tyrol, the Sanctuary of the Madonna delle Grazie near Mantua and the Waffensammlung in Vienna, among others.

## Re-enactment

Across Europe, there are numerous groups of medieval re-enactors that focus their activities on the warfare of the 14th and 15th centuries. These include not only groups re-enacting armoured warriors, archers and artillery but also re-enactors who put on displays about camp life during this period. Many of these would be of interest to any reader interested in the condottieri.

There are also several groups whose activities specifically relate to the condottieri. These include re-enactors who concentrate on various periods between 1300 and 1500. Some of these groups are dedicated to re-enacting early, non-Italian, condottieri while others re-enact Italian companies of the 15th century.

These condottieri re-enactment societies include groups such as the 'Compagnia del Fiore d'Argento' (www.silverflower.org), the 'Gesellschaft Des Elefanten' (www.company-elefant.com) and 'Mercenari del Sale' (www.storiaviva.it). There is also a condottieri re-enactor web-ring that includes links to several condottieri re-enactment groups: 'Condottieri Mauriziani 1475' (www.condottieri.at).

For the majority of collectors, Italian armour of this period would simply be beyond their price range. Occasionally pieces do come up at auction at some of the larger auction houses. There are also numerous armourers who make reproductions of Italian medieval armour. These include not only armour for the re-enacting community but also display items to museum-quality standards.

**A 15th-century illustration of handgunners from the *Rudimentum Noviciorum* (Lubeck, 1475). Here they are shown firing their weapons, touching them off with pieces of smouldering match. The illustration suggests that two different-calibre weapons are being fired.**

# GLOSSARY

| | |
|---|---|
| **arquebus** | a primitive but effective early firearm which incorporated a spring-loaded lock that brought ignited match to set off the main charge. The soldiers who used them were referred to as arquebusiers |
| ***bandiera*** | term used to describe a condottieri band or company |
| **bombard** | also referred to as a '*bombarde*', this was an early mortar-type piece of artillery, often used in sieges |
| ***caporale*** | junior leader of condottieri, usually responsible for a single lance of men |
| ***carroccio*** | horse- or ox-drawn cart used on the battlefield as command post, rallying point and fire platform. It was decorated with the state flag of an army, and its loss in battle usually signalled defeat |
| ***casa*** | (plural *case*). In civilian terms, this refers to a household. The term was also used to describe a condottieri band or company |
| ***collaterale*** | (plural *collaterali*). State official employed to oversee the administration of condottieri companies |
| ***condotta*** | (plural *condotte*). Contract, or more specifically a contract employing mercenaries. The term '*condotte*' was also later used to describe a condottieri band |
| ***condottiere*** | (plural *condottieri*). This term literally translates as 'contractor'. It referred to all who signed or were included in a state contract or *condotta*. It was later applied just to leaders of mercenaries |
| ***contado*** | the agricultural hinterland of an Italian city state |

| | |
|---|---|
| *corazza* | a small group or lance of armoured cavalry or infantry/heavy cavalry and infantry |
| **lance** | the smallest unit of a condottieri company. It could number from three to five men and was commanded by a *caporale* |
| *perpunto* | a popular type of quilted soft armour. The term was also used for a form of civilian tunic |
| *podestà* | official hired by an Italian state to govern its affairs. The *podestà*'s guard often formed the basis for later condottieri companies |
| *quastatori* | the 'devastators'. These were peasants who were employed by condottieri to despoil the territory of an enemy |
| *schiopetto* | an early and primitive type of Italian handgun. The *schiopettieri* were the handgunners who used them |
| *signori* | the *signori* were high state officials, sometimes of the aristocracy, who ruled Italian states. This system was open to abuse and could lead to a single individual acquiring the power to rule the state |
| *stradiotti* | Greek or Albanian light horsemen who were employed in condottieri armies from the 1470s |

# BIBLIOGRAPHY

Ady, C. M., *History of Milan under the Sforza*, London (1907)

Browning, Oscar, *Life of Bartolomeo Colleoni*, London (1891)

——, *The Age of the Condottieri*, London (1895)

Burkhardt, Jacob, *The Civilization of the Renaissance*, New York and London (1944)

Carferro, William, *Mercenary Companies and the Decline of Siena*, Baltimore (1998)

Collison-Morley, L. M., *The Story of the Sforzas*, London (1932)

Deiss, J. J., *Captains of Fortune*, London (1966)

Fowler, Kenneth, *Medieval Mercenaries: The Great Companies*, Oxford (2001)

Gottfried, Robert, *Doctors and Medicine in Medieval England, 1340–1530*, Princeton (1986)

Hibbert, Christopher, *Florence: The Biography of a City*, London (1993)

Hutton, E., *Sigismondo Malatesta*, London (1906)

Mallett, Michael, *Mercenaries and their Masters: Warfare in Renaissance Italy*, London (1974)

Nicolle, David, *Italian Medieval Armies, 1300–1500*, Oxford (1983)

——, *Italian Militiaman, 1260–1392*, Oxford (1999)

Norwich, John Julius, *A History of Venice*, London (1982)

Oman, Charles, *A History of the Art of War in the Middle Ages*, London (1924)

Rawcliffe, Caroline, *Medicine and Society in Medieval Europe*, Stroud (1995)

Saunders, Frances Stonor, *Hawkwood: Diabolical Englishman*, London (2004)

Sismondi, J. C. L., *History of the Italian Republics in the Middle Ages*, London (1906)

Temple-Leader, John and Giuseppe Marcotti, *Sir John Hawkwood: Story of a Condottiere*, London (1889)

Trease, Geoffrey, *The Condottieri: Soldiers of Fortune*, London (1970)

de Vries, Kelly, *Medieval Military Technology*, New York (1992)

Waley, Daniel, *The Italian City Republics*, London (1961)

Young, Peter, *The Fighting Man*, London (1981)

Ziegler, Philip, *The Black Death*, New York (1971)

# COLOUR PLATE COMMENTARY

## A: ARMOURED CONDOTTIERE, ITALIAN STYLE, EARLY 14TH CENTURY

During the 14th century mail armour still provided the main form of protection for both mounted and dismounted condottieri. The armour of the main figure is in the Italian style and is based on an effigy in Bologna dating from around 1315. This knight is depicted holding his great helm; under this he would also have worn the bascinet helmet with attached mail aventail shown here. His torso is well protected by a mail hauberk and a coat of plates. Beneath the sleeves of his hauberk this condottiere wears splint arm defences, and his hands are covered with plate-lined gauntlets. His knees are protected by leather poleyns and the lower legs by hardened leather greaves. Scale armour on the feet completes his protection. He carries his shield slung across his back, and chains secure both his sword and dagger to his belt. This relatively simple combination of mail, plate and hardened leather armour provided good overall protection. Other items include: (1) a bascinet helmet with bretache faceguard (open), and (2) a bascinet helmet, with bretache faceguard (closed); (3) an alternative method for suspending the sword based on the da Fogliano mural in Siena. The sword itself is based on the sword excavated in 1921 from the tomb of Can Grande della Scala in Verona; (4) a composite crossbow; (5) a visored great helm; (6) a helmet based on a surviving Italian example of a great helm dating from c.1300; (7) a bascinet helmet with an extra flap of mail attached over the aventail; (8) a visorless bascinet helmet.

## B: CONDOTTIERI RECRUITMENT, MID-15TH CENTURY

Although it is easy to dismiss the condottieri as being mere mercenaries, the elaborate nature of their contracts created a unique system in which the relationship between the employer and the condottiere was quite sophisticated. Each condottieri captain or captain-general would sign his contract or *condotta* in the presence of state officials and a legal notary. The state, republic or commune that employed him would be represented by one or more of the civil administration, which in turn was made up of members of the affluent merchant classes. The state government, represented by the figure here dressed in red to the left, would provide the funds necessary to pay their condottieri army. The *collaterale*, shown here in civilian costume to the right, was a legal official appointed by the state to oversee the recruiting and administration of condottieri companies. It was the responsibility of the notary (seated) to draft the elaborate *condotta* and this would include articles that defined period and terms of service. On some occasions the *condotta* made provision for pensions in the event of condottieri being severely injured. After the *condotta* was signed, it was the responsibility of the condottieri captain to have his men adequately trained and ready to serve the state that employed him. Payment for these contracts was in gold or silver coin, and condottieri could supplement their wages by looting the property of defeated enemies. The figures here are depicted wearing civilian dress or armour from the period 1435–45. In the background, two condottieri engage in sword practice; the figure to the left is wearing a leather brigandine and a mail shirt, while the right-hand figure is protected with a padded *perpunto* tunic.

## C: CONDOTTIERI COLUMN ON THE MARCH, LATE 14TH CENTURY

One of the most prominent and successful condottieri leaders was the Englishman Sir John Hawkwood (c.1320–94). Born in Essex, he had served as a soldier during the Hundred Years War but was left unemployed in 1360 following the Treaty of Brétigny. During his colourful and controversial mercenary career, at different times he commanded the Papal, Paduan and Florentine armies. He is shown here on the march with his troops, preceded by a trumpeter, whose trumpet flag displays his heraldic device: a shield incorporating a chevron and shell motif. This reconstruction of Hawkwood's armour is based on surviving examples of 14th-century Italian armour held in the Churburg Castle collection. Hawkwood's 'White Company' were given this title due to their highly polished armour and, while many contemporary paintings show armour painted black, the suit in this plate is shown as having been polished.

Although it is easy to associate the condottieri with armoured horsemen, many condottieri were actually infantrymen. Every condottieri army would include a large proportion of dismounted men-at-arms, crossbowmen, archers, handgunners and, later, artillery men. The foot soldiers in this plate are preceded by an armoured handgunner, carrying a primitive handgun with match attached to his belt. He is followed by an English archer wearing a simple open-faced bascinet and a padded jack. His arrows are carried in a bundle at the waist while his bow has been covered and slung over his back. Finally, a heavy infantryman brings up the rear of the file of foot soldiers. He carries a pole-arm and a large oval shield and is well armoured, wearing a combination of visored helmet, mail shirt, leather brigandine and also plate armour on his arms and legs.

## D: CONDOTTIERI TACTICS: THE BATTLE OF CASTAGNARO, 1387

During this period there were essentially two schools of condottieri tactical thought. The Sforzeschi school advocated massed, timed assaults, while the Bracceschi school was more flexible, placing great reliance on manoeuvre and the initiative of battlefield commanders. During this clash on the banks of the Adige river between the Paduan (red) and Veronese (blue) armies, both styles of tactic were used. This plate depicts the final stages of the battle as viewed from the north-east.

The Veronese army (1) began with a Sforzeschi-style attack with massed columns attacking the Paduan centre (2), and they initially enjoyed some success, pushing the Paduan

**Niccolò da Tolentino, the hero of San Romano, was commemorated in a frescoed monument in the Duomo in Florence. By Andrea del Castagno, it was completed in 1456 and mirrors Uccello's earlier monument to Sir John Hawkwood. (Author's photograph)**

forces back. While the Paduan commander, Sir John Hawkwood, initially responded to this attack in a similar style, he had retained a reserve of cavalry and mounted archers and, following the Bracceschi philosophy, he unleashed it around his right wing at the critical moment to cause mayhem in the Veronese rear (**3**). Both sides used *carroccios*; modified wagons that served as combined command platforms, fire positions and rallying points (**4** and **5**). The Paduan army had a small number of cannon that were also employed (**6**). The battle of Castagnaro was ultimately decided when Hawkood's Paduan troops overran the Veronese *carroccio* and their rear positions, illustrating how quite a simple battlefield manoeuvre could destroy an enemy that was committed to an all-out, Sforzeschi-style assault.

## E: DAILY LIFE IN CAMP, 15TH CENTURY
Many contemporary illustrations depict condottieri camps as being quite comfortable places. The terms of the *condotta* usually stipulated that a certain allowance of food and drink be provided for each condottiere. When in camp, the condottieri could also supplement their rations by hunting, as shown here. The larger and richer condottieri bands would acquire tents, furniture and any other equipment necessary for the maintenance of a comfortable life in camp.

In the foreground a knight is being helped into his armour by his squire. The suit of armour is based on a surviving example of Galeazzo d'Arco and is typical of Milanese armour from around 1450 onwards. The knight is shown here almost fully armoured; his left pauldron is on the ground before him and his armet and gauntlets are shown lying on the bench to the left. His squire wears fashionable two-colour leg hose while his doublet incorporates faux arming points at the shoulders. The trio of condottieri to the rear wear a mixture of armour and civilian dress. The crossbowman to the left wears coloured hose and a doublet based on an example shown in a painting by Pierro della Francesca. The seated condottiere facing the viewer wears a two-piece Italian-style breastplate with attached taces. The other condottiere wears a brigandine. Also present in this plate is the ubiquitous hound, examples of which appear in many contemporary scenes of camp life.

## F: THE BATTLE OF SAN ROMANO, 1432
This famous clash between Florentine and Sienese troops has been immortalized by Paolo Uccello in a series of three paintings, now split among galleries in London, Paris and Florence. Although depicted by Uccello as a vast clash between armoured horsemen, the infantry of both armies played a major role. The Florentine captain-general Niccolò da Tolentino had actually conducted a series of operations against the Sienese army throughout the early summer of 1432. The previous weeks of campaigning had involved the resupply of the besieged Montepulciano, the recapture of Linari and also an attempt to ambush and capture the Sienese commander, Francesco Piccinino. On 2 June 1432, Tolentino found the Sienese camp at San Romano near the Arno river. Having made a personal reconnaissance of the Sienese positions, he decided on an immediate attack. Sandwiched by Tolentino's force and another Florentine force led by Micheletto Attendolo, the Sienese army was routed after a hard-fought battle.

Tolentino is depicted here directing troops into battle and, after the style of Uccello, is shown wielding a weapon no more dangerous than his commander's baton of office. It was later recorded that, such was his haste to come to grips with the enemy, he neglected even to wear his helmet, and he is shown here wearing a flamboyant civilian hat with matching cloak. The Florentine cavalry are depicted galloping towards the Sienese, several of the knights wearing crests on their helmets. The Florentine army's victory at San Romano, and the campaign that preceded the battle, signalled a major negation in the power and prestige of Siena.

## G: AFTERMATH OF BATTLE, 15TH CENTURY
For seriously injured condottieri, there was little chance of effective medical intervention. Medieval surgeons could perform only a limited number of operations with any hope

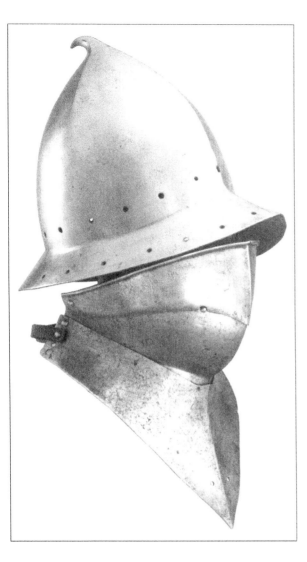

**15th-century helmet and bevor. This combination would have provided effective protection for condottieri infantrymen. (Royal Armouries, Leeds)**

The surgeon and his assistant are depicted here operating in their shirtsleeves. Some form of leather apron would also have been worn. As can be seen here, the equipment of such surgeons was primitive in the extreme and included various types of probes, knifes and cauterizing irons. Through the tent flaps, further condottieri can be seen being led forward for attention. The figure to the left wears a mail shirt and studded leather brigandine while the condottiere to the right wears an effective combination of barbuta helmet, mail shirt, breastplate and taces.

## H: ARMOURED CONDOTTIERE, LATE 15TH CENTURY

By the end of the 15th century, plate armour had developed to such a degree as to make the armoured cavalrymen almost impregnable. A considerable amount of thought had gone into developing armour that both protected the wearer and also deflected blows. Suits of armour began to sprout features designed to stop blows before they reached the main body of the suit. These features included exaggerated gardbraces that extended up over the wearer's left shoulder in an attempt to stop blows landing on the body. The Maximilian style of armour incorporated a series of fluted ribs that were designed to dissipate the force of blows.

The main figure wears a suit of full plate armour based on a surviving example dating from around 1480 in the Monastery of Santa Maria delle Grazie near Mantua. In Italy, it was still common to wear mail protection beneath such suits of plate and this figure wears both a mail shirt and a mail skirt, the fringes and sleeves of which can be seen, while further mail fringes extend beneath the knees. Mail is also attached to the end of the leg greaves to cover and protect the feet. Otherwise this condottiere is encased in plate, the front and rear views indicating not only how this suit was attached but also the massive nature of the pauldrons that protected the shoulders. This suit is shown in darkened metal rather than the highly polished style shown in Plate C. The front of the breastplate incorporates a bracket to support a lance. Also included are: (**1**) a visored armet helmet of a type depicted in a painting by Pierro della Francesca. This incorporates the sight and brow reinforcement in the visor itself rather than using the gap between the two pieces to form the sight; (**2**) a sallet helmet of the style worn by Bartolomeo Colleoni. This is in the same style as the sallet depicted on the Colleoni statue in Venice; (**3**) a 15th-century Italian armet, shown here opened up; (**4**) the barbuta helmet of the 15th-century 'Avant Armour' in Glasgow; (**5**) a late 15th-century Italian sword based on an example in the Museo Poldi Pezzoli in Milan; (**6**) an Italian brigandine based on an example preserved in Venice. This represents quite an unusual version of the brigandine as it incorporated tassets to protect the thighs; (**7**) 15th-century Italian sabatons that could also be used to protect the feet in place of mail coverings. At (**8**), in the bottom right are three figures illustrating the use of the arming doublet. The figure to the right attaches his leg harness while the middle figure shows how the mail skirt was worn. Finally, the figure to the left has put on a mail shirt over the mail skirt and now is ready to attach the suit of plate over this.

of success and it was only in the centuries that followed that we see the further medical research that led to the birth of modern medicine. While some medieval universities had established schools of medicine and surgery, Western medical theory was nowhere near as sophisticated as its Arabic and Oriental counterparts. Minor sword or arrow wounds could perhaps be treated with success. Medieval accounts also refer to amputations, and these often resulted in the death of the patient. Wounds like depressed fractures and abdominal puncture wounds represented certain death. On campaign, it would appear that condottieri columns sometimes travelled with their own surgeons, who were assisted by younger apprentice surgeons. In other cases, the surgeons and apothecaries of local towns were used to provide medical assistance after a battle.

# INDEX

References to illustrations are shown in **bold**. Plates are shown with page and caption locators in brackets.